Also by Byron Edgington:

Winner of the 2012 Bailey Prize for non-fiction from
The Swedenborg Foundation Press

Books:*
The Sky Behind Me, A Memoir of Flying and Life

SkyWriting: Essays On the Art & Craft of Aviation

A Vietnam Anthem: What the War Gave Me

Waiting For Willie Pete, a Novel of Vietnam

*Available at www.byronedgington.com

Articles published in: Vietnam Magazine, Parents Magazine, Flying, JEMS, Hospital Aviation, AOPA Magazine, Flight Journal, The IOWAN Magazine, and others.

POSTFLIGHT

Copyright © 2021 Byron Edgington
All rights reserved.

No part of this publication may be reproduced, distributed, or transmitted in any form or by any means, including photocopying, recording, or other electronic or mechanical methods, without the prior written permission of the publisher, except in the case of brief quotations embodied in critical reviews, and certain other noncommercial uses permitted by copyright law.

For permission requests, write to the publisher, addressed "Attention: Permissions Coordinator," at the address below.

ISBN: 9978-1-952779-96-1
Library of Congress Control Number: 2021910847

Cover design and layout by Manuel Serna
Author photo: www.ctw-photography.com Coralville Iowa

Published by The SkyWriter Press in the United States of America

The SkyWriter Press
281 Danielle Street
Iowa City Iowa 52245

www.Byronedgington.com

POSTFLIGHT:
AN OLD PILOT'S LOGBOOK
TIPS FOR PILOTS, AND THOSE
WHO WISH TO BE

Whatever your ambition is.....
Dream it, Believe it, Do it!
-Mandy Hickson, RAF (ret) author of An Officer, Not a Gentleman

BYRON EDGINGTON, ATP

To Mariah: soulmate, best friend, wing-person, editor, thank you for every takeoff and landing, and for your beautiful energy. Journey well!

ACKNOWLEDGEMENTS

Like every other interconnected person on this planet, as a pilot I could never have had my amazing career alone. I may have soloed on June 27th 1969, but that solo flight lasted all of 10 minutes. I must thank people who reached out to help, not only in my aviation career, but in this writing endeavor as well. Mariah, my precious wife, the 'wind-beneath-my-wings' analogy may be overused, but it applies. Others in the creation and delivery of *Postflight* include Capt. Linda Pauwels, Patty Wagstaff, Capt. Karlene Petitt, Capt. Judy Rice, Capt. Stephen Walton, Capt. Patty Bear, Capt. Rydel Pépin, Eric Noel, Anh-Thu Nguyen, Lynsey Howell, Penny Rafferty-Hamilton PhD, Randy Mains, James Thomas Fletcher, Connie Shelton, Cmdr. Jim Tritten, Capt. Bill Collier, Colten Christopher Fronk, Shannon Huffman-Polson, Mandy Hickson, Jessica Webster, Courtney Robson, and MayCay Beeler. To my contributors, my long-ago OSU journalism Prof. Tom O'Hara, (no semicolons!), Debra Cleghorn, Pamela Almand, and all who shared their hard-won aviation wisdom. And of course, Jacqueline Camacho-Ruiz, Michele Kelly, Scarlett Magaña Singh, Gaby Hernández-Franch, Juan Pablo Ruiz (great cover, espectacular!), and Karen Dix at Fig Factor Media for making *Postflight: An Old Pilot's Logbook* the work I envisioned. Anyone I failed to mention, please forgive the old pilot, he doesn't remember as well as he used to. Thank you from my heart. Journey well, my friends.

Flying, Freedom, Wings
Loved ones from across the world
Beauty connection
—Haiku by Kristin Sito CTI, Millington TN

From *Beyond Haiku, Pilots Write Poetry*
By Captain Linda Pauwels CKA MIA

Praise for Postflight

I was a first generation pilot so I could have used this book!
—**Colten Christopher Fronk**

Filled with insights and true tales of near catastrophes.
—**Jim Tritten,** Commander U.S. Navy (ret)

Every pilot will find something that speaks to them in Postflight. For me, it was the simple story of flying solo for the first time—when your flight instructor climbs out and says "take it up on your own." Sheer magic! For anyone with a dream of an aviation career, Edgington's book shares the highs and lows (literal and mental) involved in this life.
—**Connie Shelton,** Mystery writer, and world record high altitude balloon pilot.

If you believe flying is your calling, this is a must read book. Edgington's experience straddles military, civilian, medical, and business aviation. Retiring after forty years and 12,500 hours of flying, he has stories to tell, as he helps you discover pathways to flight, and the realities of getting there.
—**James Thomas Fletcher,** Author of Roses for the Canyon

Postflight: An Old Pilot's Logbook documents over 4 decades of personal knowledge, tips and stories, but this book offers you much more than that. It includes stories and anecdotes passed along from other experienced aviators as well, so you can learn from their time in the cockpit. This book is a must-read if you're interested in learning from those who have 'been there, done that' because if heeded, their experiences will make your career in aviation much safer.

—**Randy Mains,** author of *Antenna Up, Crew Resource Management for Helicopter Pilots*

Interesting, and innovative, and fun to read, with lots of good advice, especially for young women.

—**Patty Wagstaff,** Aerobatic pilot, inductee Hall of Fame, U.S. Aerobatic Team member.

Postflight is a helpful and easy read which will be of interest to many in aviation. Vietnam veterans, military and helicopter pilots, flight instructors, and those just beginning their flight plan will all find helpful information in this book.

—**Penny Rafferty Hamilton,** Ph.D., author of America's Amazing Airports: Connecting Communities to the World and Inspiring Words for Sky and Space Women: Advice from Historic and Contemporary Trailblazers.

Postflight: An Old Pilot's Logbook speaks to the adage by Dale Carnegie, "Books are a wonder. For the matter of a few dollars a man will offer up a lifetimes' experience and insight." Herein is a lifetime that exposes the mindset, decision-making, and perseverance that contribute to a successful career in aviation. The book explores the various paths a pilot might take, and the personalities that might be encountered along the way. It expands on much of the core spirit that makes aviation a truly unique endeavor.

—**Capt. Stephen Walton,** (ret) American Airlines

"There I was" stories are a tradition almost as central to aviation as planes. Adventures in the skies and sometimes on the ground populate many a post-flight gathering. Due to the nature of aviation, tragic stories mingle easily beside triumphant ones. They keep company too, with humorous, bawdy, prophetic, and warning tales. Though you will always find a pilot at the center of these stories, what those outside the profession rarely notice is that every story offers some lesson about hubris or humility, precision or sloppiness, expected and unexpected emergencies, and best and worst practices. No matter how casually offered, the ritual of storytelling among pilots passes on some vital knowledge soaked up by the brotherhood and sisterhood of the sky. Any experienced pilot will tell you there's no such thing as a perfect flight, and the best pilots will tell you they learn something new each flight. The author tells his stories and those of other pilots in the

time-honored tradition of passing on hard-won lessons. Whether you are a new or aspiring pilot, or a grey-haired experienced one, there are nuggets of wisdom slathered generously throughout this book.

—**Patty Bear,** former military pilot, retired 777 captain, author of *From Plain to Plane: My Mennonite Childhood, a National Scandal, and an Unconventional Soar to Freedom*

This book is definitely a must read for fellow pilots or pilot wannabes. His multi-faceted stories and flight training experiences are hilariously relatable. As an advocate for Asian Women in Aerospace & Aviation, I have a profound appreciation for his thorough understanding and explanation of the traditional challenges and rewards presented to women pilots and that our mission to be at the controls is synonymous to the freedom to navigate our lives.

—**Anh-Thu Nguyen,** CFI, CFII, MEI, ATP, Georgia Tech Ph.D. Candidate

---

Absolutely a wealth of insight into how unique an aviator's experience can be. From the importance in selecting a flight training provider, to developing an appreciation for precision flying, there are many great elements of how a successful aviator thinks. The extensive use of real-life flying examples to articulate complex concepts is remarkably well done. Whether you haven't touched an aircraft, or are a thousand hours into your career, there is something to be gained.

—**Eric Noel,** Director of Pilot Development, AeroGuard Flight Training Center

Postflight: An Old Pilot's Logbook is written in the spirit of aviation being for everyone, as it should be. As Byron astutely reminds us, aircraft do not know the gender of the pilot, and being in command of an aircraft grants us the agency that we should all be afforded as competent aviators. This book is an uplifting way to encourage us to pull up the generation of flyers that are coming after us.

—**Jessica Webster,** Hera Aviation Group

Incredibly well written! The author pulls together life experiences, lessons learned, and ignites the passion of taking to the sky. Not only is this a fun read, the author offers guidance, references, and paves the path to success. He's even inspired me to obtain a helicopter rating. A must read for future and current aviators alike.

—**Capt. Karlene Petitt PhD.** Typed: A350, B777, A330, B747-400, B747-200, B767, B757, B737, B727. Author of *Flight To Success, be the Captain of Your Life,* and the *Aviation "Flight For"* Thriller Series.

I strongly encourage you to further recognize yourself in reading Postflight: An Old Pilot's Logbook. It's never too early or too late to begin taking command of your life.

—**Capt. Judy Rice**

How often do you steer away from taking on a new challenge or experience because you're worried you might fail? I'm sure we're all guilty of this at some point in our lives, but until you try you never know what you are good at. Once you have a goal to visualize, it's always easier to work towards it, to focus on it. So whatever your ambition is.....Dream it, Believe it, Do it!

—**Mandy Hickson**, RAF fast-jet pilot (ret), author of *An Officer, Not a Gentleman*

The successful women pilots I've surveyed have three things in common: They have confidence, they faced their fears, and they had a great support system. I tell dads, grandfathers, brothers, uncles, encourage girls to fly. Take them to the airport, and air shows, and show them women in the cockpit.

—**Lynsey Howell ATP**, pilot, mentor, career coach, author of *Finding Amelia*

POSTFLIGHT:
AN OLD PILOT'S LOGBOOK

TABLE OF CONTENTS

Foreword: Capt. Linda Pauwels B787 Check Airman......... 18

CHAPTER 1—MY DREAM OF FLIGHT

If you have the slightest chance to fly, jump on it like a duck on a June bug. Like the isobars on weather charts, there are no straight lines leading into aviation. 19

CHAPTER 2—STUDENT PILOT

Your training will be hard, exhausting, discouraging—and triumphant! Like my summer of '69...................................... 27

CHAPTER 3—WHERE TO START

I'll give you good advice, and great resources. Trust your gut, and you'll decide well... 35

CHAPTER 4—FIXED WING?

What aircraft do you want to fly? Here are reasons to stay in airplanes.. 43

CHAPTER 5—ROTARY WING?

Flying is heavenly; hovering is divine. Or you can do both! 55

CHAPTER 6—TRANSITION: Military to Commercial

Your training will be hard, exhausting, discouraging—and triumphant! 65

CHAPTER 7—STRETCHING THE RULES

I hope you don't need this chapter, but you might. Safety first; but land safely, every time!.. 83

CHAPTER 8—SA: SITUATIONAL AWARENESS

Probably the most important asset you have–SA improves with experience. 93

CHAPTER 9—HIGH POINTS

I hope you have at least as many sublime moments flying as I did. 101

CHAPTER 10—LOW POINTS

I hope you have none of these, though I know you will. The lowest point? Your final approach and landing. I hope your career is longer than mine was. 117

CHAPTER 11—CARE & FEEDING OF YOUR MECHANIC

The wrench-benders and spark-chasers are your best friends 129

CHAPTER 12—CARE & FEEDING OF PASSENGERS

I want you to remember the folks who trust you, and I know you will. 139

CHAPTER 13—CARE & FEEDING OF YOU

Take care of yourself. Eat well; sleep well; exercise; meditate; take time off. Your career will be better 151

CHAPTER 14—CARE & FEEDING OF YOUR CREW

Care and feeding of your crew. Crew Resource Management Aviation thrives on systems. CRM will keep you safe. 163

CHAPTER 15—CARE & FEEDING OF YOUR CAREER

From start to finish, these are ways into the cockpit that will set you apart.. 175

CHAPTER 16—CONFESSIONS, STORIES, VOICES OF EXPERIENCE

Listen to my colleagues as they tell on themselves and learn from them. 193

CHAPTER 17—YES, YOU CAN FLY

Yes, you can, and these pilots back me up. Here are amazing stories from people who were starting out once, just like you... 225

CHAPTER 18—FINAL REMARKS................................... 241
Tips from Your Co-Pilots 242
Lesson Roundup 256
Resources.. 267

FOREWORD

When fellow pilot and aviation author Byron Edgington asked me to write the foreword to *Postflight*, I imagined it was due to our shared love of both aviation and writing. Then I realized, not without some chagrin, that after more than three decades flying big metal, I too had become an *Old Pilot*.

It's difficult to pinpoint the moment one is bitten by the aviation bug. When it happens, as Edgington writes of his own experience, flying becomes as much a part of us as breathing. Perhaps it's because the feeling of mastery resulting from a precise, disciplined interaction between human and machine can also yield an intangible, ephemeral connection that touches the spiritual realm.

In pilot speak, *Postflight* is good gouge.

Replete with real life anecdotes and lessons learned, often the hard way, *Postflight: An Old Pilot's Logbook* is a genuine dose of hangar flying for aspiring pilots and aviation enthusiasts alike. Read it and you'll fully understand the saying "there are old pilots, and there are bold pilots, but there are no old bold pilots."

—Captain Linda Pauwels, B787 Check Airman and author of *Beyond Haiku: Pilots Write Poetry*

Chapter 1

MY DREAM OF FLIGHT

Timing
Hughes 269/TH-55, Summer '69
If you can fly one of these, you can fly the box it came in

Take opportunities to fly where you find them.

—*An old pilot*

When I was 10 years old I lived across the fence from a TV station. One afternoon I heard the telltale whop-whop-whopping sound of rotor blades. I rushed outside as the helicopter angled in on short final to the grass and landed. That was in 1958 when helicopters were rarely seen or used, so it's interesting to me today that I knew from its noise what kind of aircraft it was. A popular TV show at the time was 'Whirlybirds,' and the helicopter in that show was like the one that landed near my house, a Bell model 47, so that likely explains it. Or perhaps I was waiting to hear it, I don't know.

The pilot idled the helicopter's engine, then the passenger door opened and a fancy fellow wearing a suit stepped out. My mother told me it was Van Johnson, a popular TV and movie star at the time. Johnson had starred in such Hollywood productions as *30 seconds over Tokyo, and Brigadoon.*

To me, the real star of that day was the helicopter. I watched the pilot rev up the engine, heard the blades whop-whop a bit more with increased rpm, and then the ungainly machine lifted into the sky. I was mesmerized. I imagined myself at the controls, moving the cyclic and collective to take the aircraft aloft. I envied that pilot. I wanted to *be* that pilot. I vowed that someday, somehow, though I was just a dreamy-eyed, sky-blue collar kid, I'd become a pilot. How I'd eventually get to the cockpit never crossed my mind when I was a clueless 10-year old.

CHAPTER 1: MY DREAM OF FLIGHT

Flash forward to February 1969, when I was a clueless 21-year old. I'd been drafted into the US Army, and sent to Fort Jackson South Carolina. The second day at the reception station I was on my bunk bored and restless, a bit nervous about what my future held. Thinking my pursuit of aviation had been derailed, I was waiting for something to happen. What happened that afternoon changed my life.

With 200 other recruits I was ordered outside to stand in formation. Once there, we all looked at each other wondering what was about to transpire? I'd been in the green machine only 24 hours, but I was already familiar with the simple truth that the military doesn't tell you anything. I trooped outside, and entered the formation.

At the front, an NCO held a clipboard. He ordered us to listen up. His barked instructions were simple: A soldier who answers yes to any of these questions should leave the formation, and go back to the billet. Then the sergeant started reading off those items: *Older than 30, height more than five-ten, weight more than 220, married with more than one child, police record except traffic violations...* and on and on. As the sergeant droned on with several more qualifiers, more and more men left the formation and returned to the barracks.

Once he finished, I was left standing in line with only 15 other men. We looked at each other wondering what we'd just volunteered for? No one told us…yet. The sergeant ordered us to follow him into a small building, where desks were lined up as in a fifth-grade classroom.

On each desk was a pamphlet with 200 questions on perhaps 15 pages, and a couple of #2 pencils. We were told to take a seat, open the booklets, and complete the quiz inside. *"When you're done,"* the sergeant said. *"Take the test to Captain O'Neal, and wait."*

I flipped open the pamphlet. Based on the questions, including diagrams and multiple-choice options, I realized it was a test for flight school.[1] Timing is everything, I thought. It was 1969. The war in Vietnam was at full throttle; the army needed helicopter pilots. And there I was. I completed the test, handed it to Capt. O'Neal to be graded, and waited outside his office as I'd been told.

Minutes later, the captain called my name, and I entered his office. *"You want to fly helicopters, Edgington?"* He may as well have asked if I'd like to continue breathing. *"Absolutely,"* I said. *"Okay, go gather up your shit, and report to Sergeant Cassidy in the next building. We'll be sending you to Fort Polk for basic training where the other WOFTs will be."*

With my head in the clouds at that point, I failed to ask Capt. O'Neal what exactly a WOFT was? Forty-eight hours later I was posted at Fort Polk Louisiana and designated in

CHAPTER 1: MY DREAM OF FLIGHT

army-speak a Warrant Officer Flight Trainee, a WOFT. It appeared that I'd be spending the next several years with my head in the clouds; I was on my way to flight school.

The lesson is this: If you see the smallest, most obscure hint of an idea that you might possibly get your foot in the aviation door, jump on it like a duck on a June bug. In aviation, opportunities arrive in the strangest ways. Like the isobars on a weather chart, there are no straight lines leading into aviation. Sometimes I'm convinced that there is no front door.

I finished basic training at Fort Polk in late April 1969. Then I hopped on a bus with several other WOFTs for a trip across Texas to Fort Wolters, 50 miles west of Fort Worth. As the bus entered Wolters, it passed beneath an arch with a sign that read 'Above the Best.' Two helicopters were posted there, one on either side of the arch. Within a month I was in the cockpit of a helicopter like those at the Wolters gate with an instructor named Wayne Alexander who was doing his level best to teach me to fly.

In each chapter I'll give you a lesson I wish I'd learned when I started flying. For example, the training sessions I'll describe to you while I flew in the Texas heat, with Wayne scolding me about my incompetence, yelling at me about *Airspeed! Trim! RPM!* I'll tell you how difficult it might be at times. I'll advise you where you can start, and reinforce your gut instinct, an asset you should rely on in your journey to the cockpit. Those tense, oven-hot days with Wayne as I learned to fly were damned hard. I thought about quitting a few times. I'm glad I stuck it out, because, though I'd never imagined learning to fly the way I did, it was the best instruction I ever had.

The year of combat flying in Vietnam topped those lessons in difficulty. The war gave me more than just hours in a logbook. It gave me experience I could never have gained otherwise, and the belief that I had the ability to be a damned good pilot.[2] Beyond the 1,200 hours I flew in Vietnam, the hair-raising missions, threatening weather, and aircraft mechanical malfunctions, my year of combat flying gave me the best introduction there could be to the vagaries and unpredictability of aviation.

Here's another lesson for you: There are no 'natural pilots.' None of us were born to the sky. If we had been, we'd have been born with feathers. The reason I mention this is that, should you ever doubt your ability to fly, consider this: In the air, we're *all* out of our element. No one is supposed to be there, and but for human dreams of flight, your confidence coupled with determination, technical and engineering advances, and a lot of blood, sweat, and tears along the way, you'd still be grounded. Every pilot was where you are once. Today many thousands of

CHAPTER 1: MY DREAM OF FLIGHT

human beings, otherwise known as pilots, take to the air every day, in perfectly routine fashion. And so can you.

I flew for a year in Vietnam, returned to the states in March of '71, and endured a number of non-flying jobs while searching for a paying seat in a helicopter. It took me 10 years to find one, and my first few flying jobs were far from romantic, lucrative, or desirable.

In these chapters I'll tell you about those jobs and more. The lesson I drew from flying in combat for a year was that I was indeed a good pilot—I survived Vietnam—and that my experience level would only go up. I looked forward to spending more time in the sky, gaining experience, and filling my logbook with the intention of passing along my acquired wisdom to pilots like you coming up behind me. Inside this book are many of those tips.

Wayne, my flight instructor, was a demanding taskmaster. But his brand of teaching helped me survive Vietnam, and prepared me well for a life in aviation. I've dedicated this book to a few other people, but Wayne is near the top. One of the first things I learned from him, reinforced over 50 years, and 12,500 hours in the cockpit, is that *all* pilots have a duty to teach. As colleague Jim Dulin puts it: I cannot *not* teach.

Lessons:

- Take opportunities to fly when and where you find them.
- Never doubt your own ability.
- Find a tough instructor.
- Show up ready to commit aviation.
- Timing is everything.

—An old pilot

Chapter 2
STUDENT PILOT

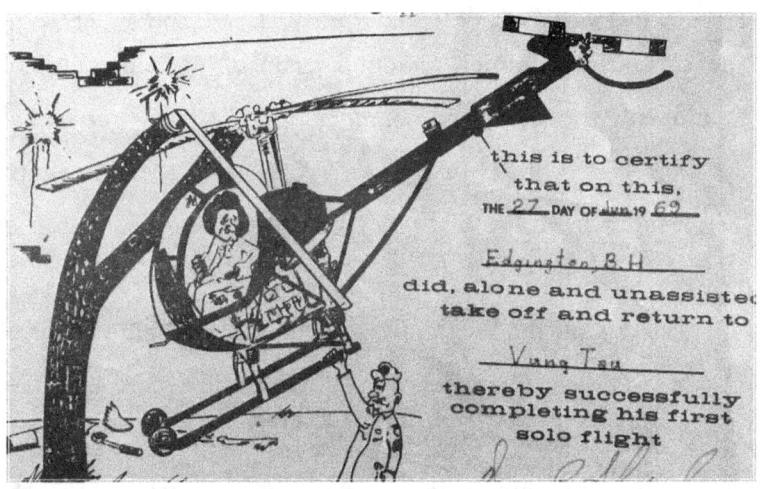

Solo: June 27th 1969

To fly solo in this hyper-protective world is almost too rewarding.

—*An old pilot*

My instructor pilot in flight school was a burly, highly profane Texan named Wayne Alexander. Wayne seemed to believe that god's last name was *'Dammit.'* He had an aggressive teaching style that included smacking the side of my flight helmet with a yellow #2 pencil when I screwed up, which happened a lot. If I didn't perform to his liking—I'd shoot past an altitude, or drift out of trim, or botch an easy landing—the next thing I'd see would be yellowish pencil shards clouding the cockpit, a hammering sound against my helmet, (thank goodness I wore one!) and *"G...dammit, Edgington I got a whole lot more screwin' to do, and you're tryin't kill me!"* In the sultry Texas summer of 1969, Wayne Alexander broke a shit ton of yellow #2 pencils.

But he taught me to fly the squirrely, unforgiving little Hughes 269 helicopter, and once I'd flown a few more aircraft—the UH-1 Huey, an AS-350 AStar, several versions of the Bell 206, a CH-47 Chinook among others—I can safely say that the Hughes was the most difficult to learn to fly. By choosing the Hughes as an ab initio training aircraft, the Army had picked the right machine to weed out anyone who might be aviation deficient. If you can fly a Hughes 269, you can fly the box it came in. From my starting flight school class of 250 students, half of us graduated.

Wayne and I would launch into the hot Texas afternoon,

CHAPTER 2: STUDENT PILOT

and the harassment would start right away: *"More pedal! Check your altitude! Trim! RPM!"* Pencil shavings flying, rivers of sweat tickling my sides, I'd do my best to keep the helicopter under a semblance of control, while doing whichever maneuver Wayne ordered me to do. His vulgar pronouncements referencing my airmanship—or lack of it—would have been disheartening and defeating had I taken them personally. But I didn't. I heard that Wayne treated all his student pilots the same; it was just his style. His favorite expression concerning my feeble attempt to master the aircraft was, *"Edgington, you're a day late and a dollar short!"*

Then one day, the day I would solo, I understood why Wayne's harassment, his foul language, and the broken pencils mattered. It all came together, not just the flying but my personal insight. I remembered that guy flying the Bell 47 in my backyard when I was a kid. I remembered the pilot dropping off that movie star, and revving the helicopter's engine, and then lifting into the azure sky. I remembered wanting to *be* that pilot. I sat in the cockpit that day in Texas and realized that I'd become that pilot. I had my hands on the controls, my feet on the pedals, just like he had. Sauntering off like that movie star did when I was ten, Wayne walked away, leaving me to fly alone.

It was Friday, June 27, 1969, and hotter than a honeymoon mattress. I'd had a reasonably stable session with Wayne.

He'd even given me an indirect compliment after my practice autorotation: *"Edgington, you might've actually survived that one."* I took the snarky comment in stride and kept flying.

After we'd been airborne for thirty minutes, Wayne pointed toward the base of the small tower at the stage field. *"Land right over there,"* he said. So, I did. As soon as I brought the throttle back to idle, Wayne unbuckled his seat belt, and stepped out of the cockpit. I figured he had to take a leak, or maybe he had a hot screwin' date, or something. But that wasn't it. He secured his loose seat belt inside the aircraft, mashed the intercom button, and said, *"Give me three laps around the traffic pattern, and land back here."* My heart rate clipped right up to frantic. *I'm gonna solo!* I watched Wayne walk away. *Holy buckets! I'm gonna solo!* Then he wandered back to the aircraft, and plugged his mic cord in. *"Remember, it's gonna fly different without my fat ass in it."* He walked away again.

The revelation came suddenly, but with a clarity I'd never sensed before, nor possibly since. It was the reason I'd wanted to fly: My fate, my aspirations, and my vector in life were literally in my own hands. No matter how my looming solo flight went, regardless of how well or poorly I did in training going forward, I was in control of it. If I screwed up, there'd be no Wayne Alexander jumping in to rescue me, no ceding control to some other entity—a god, or an autopilot, or a committee rushing in

CHAPTER 2: STUDENT PILOT

to save my sorry ass. I was the pilot; I was in command of my life and my fate.

The revelation showed something else, something I never anticipated, especially after I'd completed my three solo laps around the traffic pattern. It was one of the reasons that flying appealed to me as it did, the pull it had on me that was, quite literally, stronger than gravity: Precision mattered; order mattered. During my three solo trips around the patch that day, I critiqued my own performance step-by-step, minute-by-minute. With Wayne on the ground watching me fly, I replaced his criticizing and grading behavior with my own. Alone in the cockpit, exact altitude became important to me. *Five hundred feet, not four-fifty!* I scolded myself. If the trim ball lazed half a width off, it bothered me: *'Trim, dammit!'* If engine rpm sagged fifty, or even twenty rpm, I corrected it: *'Check RPM!'*

I understood one reason why aviation appealed to me so much. Having been raised in a chaotic, one might say 'imprecise' home as the second of 10 kids, I'd been seeking precision and order, harmony and predictability for quite a while. Flying solo that day showed me what precision meant. I liked it. And I had complete control over it. The ramifications were exciting. So, when Wayne stepped out of the cockpit that day, another pilot stepped in. That pilot was me.

I took off. Solo. Alone in the cockpit. For some reason all

of Wayne's vulgarity, his projectile pencils, and his screaming dissatisfaction evaporated and I remembered what he'd taught me. I lifted off, alone, flew around the traffic pattern three times, and landed. I may not have been the world's best pilot at that moment, but I was a pilot.

Something else occurred to me. Wayne's job in the summer of 1969 was not so much to get me and his other students through flight school. That was only a part of his assignment. Wayne's other job was to identify individuals who simply couldn't hack the program: The difficult conditions, the steep learning curve, and the constant verbal and physical pummeling; the literal and figurative heat. If we couldn't take the heat in Texas, we sure as hell wouldn't survive the cauldron of Vietnam, a destination that drew closer every day. In South Asia it would be considerably hotter, in every way imaginable.

When I arrived in Vietnam in March 1970 and started hearing more than pencil impacts against my helmet, hearing the screams of injured men, sweating till I was soaked through from fear and the Vietnamese climate, I understood that Wayne's harsh and demanding style of instruction had been entirely appropriate.[3]

Within a month of my arrival in Vietnam, I was flying combat missions with the company, a so-called 'lift unit' of the 101st Airborne Division. As a 'peter-pilot,' that is, a rookie, I was

CHAPTER 2: STUDENT PILOT

assigned to the right seat of the Huey, while the veteran pilot, the Aircraft Commander, (AC), occupied the left seat. It didn't take long for me to realize, yet again, the value of precision. The ACs had it. I did not. Yet. I vowed to become an aircraft commander as soon as possible.

During the two months I was a peter-pilot, I needed to log sufficient hours to move into the left seat, in order to be assigned my own Huey and crew and become an aircraft commander. My need for precision, and my focus on flying as safely and predictably as possible could be—probably would be—my ticket to survival in combat. Once I'd flown 180 hours in Vietnam, I received my aircraft commander orders, and moved into the left seat of UH-1H 68-16252. I was then in command of not only the helicopter and its crew but I was also in charge of my own fate.

Here's hoping you earn that left seat yourself and take charge of your own life. No aircraft recognizes gender differences, but every aircraft rewards competence. The sky is plenty big enough for all of us.

Lessons:
- Becoming a pilot is worth it, but only if you believe it is.
- To solo an aircraft in this hyper-protective world is almost too rewarding.
- A life in aviation isn't easy, predictable, romantic, or enriching, at least in terms of dollars, but you'll never regret it.
- Precision is the mark of an aviator. Strive for it.
- Remember, you're always a student.

—An old pilot

Chapter 3
WHERE TO START

On the Khe Sanh Airstrip January 1971

Author on the left/CC Gil Alvorado right, UH-1H 68-16252 in the middle

Fly aircraft with your head, not your hands and feet.

—*An old pilot*

You've decided you will fly, that nothing will stop you, and the sooner you can start training the better. So, where to start? There are a number of good flight schools, numerous resources out there, and an almost overwhelming number of hard-sell, on-line sites that can paralyze and confuse you as to which is better, or cheaper, or more convenient, or faster. Once you start researching sites online, the pilot training ads will start pouring into the computer as the algorithm identifies your interest.

One way to start down the road to an aviation career may be to go low tech at first. Start by asking pilots, go to airports, gather opinions, and perspectives, and testimonials both good and bad. As mentioned in chapter one: There are very few straight lines leading to your goal. There are as many paths toward an aviation career as there are aviators.

But certainly, the first step is the most important one: Make sure you're physically capable of becoming a pilot. If you have a physical or medical challenge of any kind, it's best to find out early. Gaining medical clearance will be an ongoing factor in your career until the last day you fly. This is a good reason to have a backup plan.

If you can't obtain a medical clearance for the type of flying you wish to pursue, you'll need to either obtain a waiver, or fly a lower classification of aircraft.

CHAPTER 3: WHERE TO START

Medical certificates,[4] commonly referred to simply as "the medical", come in three classes: class 1, 2, and 3. The class 1 medical is the certificate required for flying scheduled operations under either federal air regulations (FAR) Part 121 or 127. Commercial pilots operating under FAR Part 135, commonly referred to as charter pilots, must have a class 2 medical. Private pilots flying under FAR Part 91 need only a class 3 medical. Student and recreational pilots are also required to have a 3rd class medical.

The FAA website details medical certification requirements, including acquisition of medicals, time limits of each, physically limiting conditions, waivers to certificates if warranted, and various other FAQs. For more information, check the FAA website.

Here's a fact that you as a rookie or potential pilot need to know, and it may be the best-kept secret in aviation: Flying isn't that difficult. Once you've mastered the physical, hands-on part of manipulating the aircraft controls, and once you can competently take the machine into the sky and land it with little or no mayhem, it doesn't get harder, it gets easier. There are numerous pilots working in aviation today who are marginally competent. These pilots put in their time, day after day, meet the schedule, take off and land reasonably well, and keep the passengers happy and alive. These pilots may have gotten Cs and maybe a few Ds in school, but they pass FAA and company line checks, and are able to keep their certificates, despite having C or D level skills.

The point is, don't doubt your ability. With reasonable finesse and average intelligence, plus a bit of common sense, you can be a pilot. At the end of the book, I list schools that can get you started. There are several more, so do your homework, ask around, don't assume it's too difficult, or beyond your capacity. Barring a physical or emotional limitation, you can fly if you have the desire and motivation to do it.

RESOURCES TO ACQUIRE AVIATION SKILLS

Aircraft Owner's and Pilot's Association: (AOPA[5]): is an excellent resource for information, including an on-line survey for flight school selection.

https://www.aopa.org/learntofly/school/Aopa.org/800-872-2672

Flying clubs: Flying clubs can be inexpensive ways to learn to fly, especially if the club has a flight instructor available.

Gateway Programs:[6] These flight training programs are common in Europe and Asia and are starting to appear in the US. A few airlines sponsor them as a way to train and hire their own pilots. 'JetBlue Gateway Select' is an example of one such program. United Airlines' Aviate[7] program is another. Another one is through Miami-Dade College. There are several similar degree-granting schools.

<u>Local Fixed-Base Operator:</u> (FBO): Some local airports house a FAR Part 61 flight training section, with instructors on staff. Prices vary and taking lessons there may be less satisfying than those offered at a Part 141 school, but there can be advantages as well, such as flying with the same instructor every time.

<u>The difference between a FAR Part 141 school and a Part 61 school is this:</u> Part 141 schools are dedicated flight schools, with their only goal of training you to fly whichever category of aircraft you choose. A Part 61 school is commonly located with the FBO at your local airport. A Part 61 school's function is also flight training, but that training is simply a part of the overall flying business at the FBO. Think of it as attending a culinary school vs. working in a combination restaurant, travel agency, and drug store. Both schools can teach you to fly, but the Part 141 school, with somewhat more FAA oversight and a strict flight-training curriculum, may better suit your needs. Plus, you can gain certifications quicker, with fewer hours flown, in a Part 141 school.

<u>An addendum to the FBO method:</u> Look for empty seats. I learned to fly fixed-wing aircraft at a local FBO that had a mission slated to depart at 6 a.m. every day, for one hour of flight time. The pilot, who was an instructor, took off solo, flew the assigned flight, and returned. I asked if I could ride along, agreeing to pay for the instructor's time, to take lessons to and from the site of the contract. The operator agreed, since the empty seat was going along anyway. It was a win-win for both of us. I logged one hour each day, performed a takeoff and landing, and practiced emergency procedures and maneuvers to and from the site, and learned to fly in a Cessna 182 RG for $14 an hour!

Buy your own aircraft: Though relatively expensive, buying your own airplane or helicopter, then hiring an instructor, can be a method of training, especially if you intend to own an aircraft eventually anyway. This could be an even better option if you form a club with other pilots and pool your resources. Aircraft ownership also offers you a chance to gain a better background in maintenance and aviation records. Trade-A-Plane is a monthly listing of all things aviation related, and a trusted industry resource for finding used aircraft, parts, insurance quotes- you name it. A qualified and trusted mechanic should look over any potential aircraft before you purchase it for its mechanical status, airworthiness, and the condition and continuity of its maintenance logs.

Lessons:

- Ask questions—veteran pilots are always happy to help.
- Make sure you're medically qualified to fly.
- Flying isn't difficult, but it demands precision.
- A flying club can be a great resource.

—*An old pilot*

Chapter 4
FIXED WING?

Cessna 182
I learned to fly FW in one of these

Side benefits are what may hold your attention and interest.

—An old pilot

Do you want to fly airplanes? Or helicopters? It can be an easy choice but isn't always. My dream was simply to fly. I managed to do that, both in the military and commercially for almost fifty years. I'd heard the exchange between fixed-wing and rotary-wing pilots, the friendly banter about which category is better, flies faster, goes higher, and all the hangar flying that takes place when pilots congregate. I'd heard fixed-wing drivers say, "Any pilot who says he doesn't want to fly for the airlines will lie about other shit, too." I was tempted once to fly for the airlines, to cruise all over the world, flirt with flight attendants, and make a bucket of money.

I'm glad I chose to fly helicopters instead. In the next two chapters I'll discuss the pros and cons of a career in each category.

FIXED-WING

I understand the attraction to airline flying: The big, fast, heavy, expensive, sophisticated equipment; the (somewhat) larger monetary reward; the envious look from people as pilots saunter through airports wearing jaunty caps, with stripes on their arms, and epaulets on their shoulders. I get that.

Unless you choose fixed-wing spraying crops, or as a bush pilot with landings and takeoffs from rough, rural, often unimproved airfields, flying fixed-wing always brings you home to a paved, well-lit, well-surveyed runway that's generally long

CHAPTER 4: FIXED WING?

and wide enough for whatever aircraft you land on it. This is one of the downsides of fixed-wing flying: You *need* a runway. If you have an in-flight issue, and landing becomes urgent, putting the plane down in Farmer Jake's bean field can be sporty and expensive.

Modern aircraft engines are extremely reliable. They're so well designed, engineered, crafted, and maintained that an engine failure is a rare occurrence. These days most pilots will finish a career without an engine failure. But then there are pilots who do abruptly end their career when an engine fails. Fortunately, regulations generally demand more than one engine for commercial operations, so it shouldn't be an issue.

There's another difference between fixed and rotary-wing, and this one benefits you as a fixed-wing pilot. It's far more common to find simulators oriented to airplanes than helicopters. As pilots climb the career ladder of the airlines, they go "to the schoolhouse" to fly the simulator on a regular basis. As a helicopter pilot, you'll rarely get that opportunity, unless you're flying in either the National Guard/Reserve or the active military, and even there simulators are rarely used.

In my career I saw the progress of aviation simulation, and those advances were impressive. When I started my career, flight simulation was crude at best. During the instrument phase of flight school, I spent several hours in what we called the "blue canoe" a crude early simulator, the Link Trainer.[8] It was a cockpit mockup with technical capability on par with a self-winding watch. After Vietnam, the Army adapted Huey cockpits, matching them up with prehistoric computerization and the rough beginnings of emergency procedures software. By the time I retired, I'd flown the $30 million CH-47 Chinook simulator with full graphics, six degrees of motion, and virtually every emergency or malfunction the real Chinook might experience stored right in the simulator's virtual brain...for transfer into mine. The use of simulators has contributed a great deal to the aviation safety record, at least the commercial fixed-wing side of it. In helicopters not so much.

The runway landing vs. off-airport landing scenario presents another consideration. Flying fixed-wing offers a more ordered, cleaner, possibly safer destination selection, albeit a more closely supervised one. Airports have more pilot amenities than a clearing in the bush 400 miles west of Godforgotit, Alaska.

Bush flying and off-airport operations may not appeal to you. Nothing wrong with that. You need to be honest with yourself. There's a lot to be said for a hot shower, clean sheets, and a good WIFI connection. If your idea of camping out is calling room service and finding the line busy, that should tell you something about your choice. Maybe fixed-wing aviation is for you.

CHAPTER 4: FIXED WING?

Another advantage of fixed over rotary-wing flying is the chance to pile hours in your logbook. I flew helicopters for fifty years and finished up with 12,500 flight hours. Had I flown fixed-wing, that number would likely be doubled, at least. I don't know what the record number of flight hours ever amassed is, but I wouldn't be surprised if it's well north of 50,000 hours.

This offers another consideration, however. Do you want to fly 30,000 hours? Or do you want to fly one hour 30,000 times? In other words, do you want a bit of variety as you take to the sky, or is cockpit experience sufficient to you? Again, being honest about what you want is important, especially if you acquire the debt that accompanies aviation training. You may find yourself stuck for a few years doing something you don't like, until you're financially able to move on. Of course, that describes several vocations.

Here's another secret for you, something airline pilots will only admit under their breath: Many of them would prefer not to fly "wet cargo," that is people. They'd prefer flying cargo aircraft instead. Especially today, as I write this, with mask-wearing mandates creating tensions in the cabin and the perception—real or not—that airline service has deteriorated, and with the myriad issues that flying real people causes, many airline pilots would rather take cargo runs. The money is the same or better, the flying can be much easier and relaxing, and schedules are often better. Especially if you're a night person, flying cargo can be a very fulfilling career.

Also, do you want to fly long-haul, transoceanic, world-straddling aircraft? Or would you rather be a 'flat-earther' in airline parlance, a pilot who flies short, busy routes, and enjoys them. Some advantages of short-leg flying are that it's a better way to hone takeoff and landing skills. It may put you back with your family more often as well, and possibly allow an upgrade sooner than later.

Sometimes the side benefits of a career are what may truly hold your attention and interest. In regard to that, fixed-wing flying may have a decided advantage for you. Flying for the airlines offers perks that rotary-wing aviation cannot such as free travel for your family etc. Once you have years of experience and seniority, airline flying can offer you fewer days at work. Fixed-wing flying, especially with an airline, offers you a more predictable work schedule as well.

As for compensation, I've heard that the airlines pay better, that there's a shortage of pilots, which bumps paychecks up a bit. But another thing I learned in aviation: As it pertains to pilot compensation—regardless of category—there's seldom a connection between supply and demand. (It's a mystery.)

Lastly, flying fixed-wing may not provide you exposure

to the maintenance aspects of aviation, especially in airline operations. This can be a plus or minus for you, depending on your viewpoint. Even in commuter operations, there's not a lot of interaction with mechanics and their magic. It all depends on the degree of exposure you want. Which leads me to the last part: The possibility that you can fly both fixed and rotary-wing.

There are flight departments in corporate aviation that require you to be current and qualified in both categories. Years ago, I was offered a position at Bendix Corporation near Detroit. At the time, the company flew a twin-engine helicopter, a Bell 222, and (if memory serves) a Sabreliner business jet. At the time I was only rotary-wing qualified. So, I was offered the helicopter job at Bendix with the proviso that I'd be trained to fly the jet at some point. For unrelated reasons I didn't accept the position, but the offer was a routine one in corporate flying. It's more likely you'll be presented with the job to fly fixed-wing with the understanding that you'll eventually learn to fly helicopters.

When I started flying commercially in 1981, by regulation a single-engine aircraft was required to have every item and system operational, or it wasn't airworthy. Those flying the big iron, the 737s, A320s, the Concordes etc. had a minimum equipment list[9] (MEL). The MEL authorized large aircraft to fly with certain specified items inoperative. It wasn't until the late '90s that helicopter operators had operations specifications (Op-Specs) to use an MEL. The change in regulations let us helicopter jockeys fly legally after hedging for a lot of years.

Another difference between a fixed-wing and a rotary-wing career is the mission itself. In the military, I flew all over the world doing all manner of missions including a year in combat. On balance, the military offered a bigger variety of jobs and much more opportunity to see the world than flying commercial helicopters did. Missions in the civilian rotary-wing world can be very interesting and extremely gratifying, but they tend to be more mundane, perhaps too much so to hold your interest. In a later chapter, I describe my flight across the state of Ohio in a Jet Ranger at thirty knots.

Flying in the corporate world could match the airlines for pay, perhaps even better it, but the flying may satisfy you less. I flew corporate for two years—the longest five years of my life. Here's my (heavily biased) description of corporate aviation: Fly the boss and his compadres from point A to point B; wait—sometimes all day—then fly them from point B back to point A. I had many long, boring days lounging in a helicopter, parked in a field, far away from anything including food, toilet facilities, or anything else for eight or ten hours, until the guys in suits returned in a hurry to get home. The equipment was superb; the pay was excellent; ditto for the bennies; I never worked a weekend; never carried a pager. I hated it.

CHAPTER 4: FIXED WING?

A plus factor to flying in the corporate world is that every assigned flight will likely be to a different location. There will be much more diversity in flight legs, often a better chance for more takeoffs and landings, somewhat less rigidity in scheduling, and obviously a smaller passenger load, often the same people every time. Flying corporate in a fractional ownership arrangement can offer the opportunity to be hired as a personal pilot for a company participating in the arrangement.

A possible negative aspect of corporate flying is that the aircraft and your pilot position will be under constant scrutiny by the bean counters. If it appears to the number crunchers that propping up the company bottom line means the flying toys have to go, then you'll be out the door as well.

It's likely that every pilot who's flown in the corporate world has a similar tale about being let go, and here's mine: When I flew in Indiana for the coal mining operation, I sensed that the company was in financial trouble, and I was right. Their primary source of income was from coal extraction and in 1981 the price of a ton of coal dropped like, well, like a rock.

One Monday morning, I reported to work, wearing my usual flying clothes expecting to fly the boss somewhere, perhaps to one of the many job sites scattered around. Sure enough, as soon as I entered the building, he called me into his office. I expected him to tell me to get the helicopter out, that he wanted to fly to one of the sites, and what time, and who was going along, etc.

Well... The first thing he said to me was, "How much do you think I can get for that helicopter?"

It was a bit disheartening to say the least. I arranged with OmniFlight, an aviation company in Janesville, Wisc. to broker the sale of the helicopter and went looking for my next seat. The good news was that OmniFlight was looking for a pilot in Iowa City, Iowa at their air medical contract. I applied for that position, got it, and didn't leave for twenty years. Aviation is indeed a very small industry.

Something else to consider, expect more structure and more adherence to rigid rules in the fixed-wing world. There's nothing wrong with structure. A set of well-defined, and well-followed systems and rules has led to a commendable safety record in the airline industry. I'm no rebel, far from it, but airline operations means always flying by committee, always waiting for the crew to key in on decisions, always following a checklist like it was your religion, which it is. If that's what floats your boat, by all means go for it. The perks really are attractive, I admit. It just wasn't my cup of java.

Other differences between the two categories come down

CHAPTER 4: FIXED WING?

to operating the aircraft. If you have no working knowledge of helicopter flight, here are a few of those differences: Taking off in an airplane requires you to raise the nose; in helicopters, it requires you to lower the nose. In a helicopter, your landing sequence is slow down, stop, land; in an airplane it's land, slow down, stop. This is a critical difference, or so I'm told.

The decision to fly either helicopters or airplanes comes down to your personal desire at some point. I knew myself well enough to understand that I might get behind an aircraft that flew faster than I could think. An anonymous jet pilot once said, "You've never been lost till you've been lost at Mach 2." I know I picked the proper category of aircraft, and my spotless safety record attests to that. I'd rather have been the best pilot at 100 knots than the worst one at 500 knots.

Something else to consider is that airplanes commonly have more range than helicopters do. The typical airplane's fuel tank can hold four, six, ten, fourteen hours of fuel or more. As soon as you take off in a helicopter, you'll be looking for a gas station. The longest legged helicopter I ever flew, the CH-47 Chinook, had enough go juice for perhaps three hours aloft, depending on its cargo weight. I have about a two-hour bladder, so even the 'Hook' was a challenge for me at times. Especially as I got older, my first stop after landing wasn't ops, the weather office, or the candy machine, it was the restroom. If you crave a

Starbucks Venti with an extra shot of caffeine before you fly, you may want to stick with the airlines. Big planes have lavatories.

Choosing to fly either fixed or rotary-wing also depends on why you chose aviation in the first place. If you're only interested in the money, the airlines are the way to go. If you want to experience the real ups and downs of aviation, and like me, you want to be alone in the cockpit, helicopters might be a better choice. In the next chapter I'll describe a few important differences.

Lessons
- Fly solo? Or as a crew? Depends on what you want.
- Fixed-wing offers more travel, time in the logbook, and (eventually) better pay.
- Many F-W pilots prefer flying cargo instead of passengers.
- It's feasible to purchase your own fixed-wing, less so a helicopter.

—*An old pilot*

Chapter 5
ROTARY-WING?

The CH-47D Chinook

To fly is human; to hover is divine.

—*Anonymous*

I had the opportunity to fly for the airlines many years ago, but I decided to stay with helicopters. I'm glad I did. Rotary-wing aviation was a perfect fit for me, and I'll never regret it. For one thing, virtually all commercial flying in helicopters is single pilot. In a military helicopter I never flew alone. I always had company up at the pointy end, and that was okay. But I preferred flying alone, that is, single pilot, if for no other reason than the higher quality of the crew experience.

I liked being *The* pilot, instead of *A* pilot. Without dipping into psychobabble, I preferred it partly because, as the second of ten kids growing up, often lost in the scrum of bodies and personalities, being *The* pilot gave me an identity and some differentiation from the crowd. I enjoyed it also because I was the one making the decisions. It was all on me whether to accept a mission or not. All on me to fly the machine, to interpret the weather, to manipulate the controls, and to manage the aircraft systems and fuel, etc. When something went wrong, it was my responsibility to deal with it correctly. It was on me to take the machine into the sky, keep my passengers and the aircraft's owners happy, and to bring it all back at the end of the day in one chunk. I liked that sense of agency.

Another personal aspect I mentioned earlier is that I think better at 100 knots. Everyone learns at a different rate and in a different fashion. I'm not a slow learner, but I'm no quick

CHAPTER 5: ROTARY-WING?

study, either. I take my time, absorb things, and wait till I have sufficient data before acting. This in itself is a useful trait in aviation. The upside is that once I've learned something, it sticks with me forever, or until I die whichever comes first.

Helicopters typically have more moving parts than airplanes, thus there's more to preflight (some say more to go wrong). Helicopter operators typically operate within a smaller profit margin, so a malfunction in a helicopter can be a bigger potential problem for your boss, thus pressure on you to fly a marginal machine could be higher as well.

As for engine malfunctions, helicopters have the advantage of a maneuver called autorotation, which allows a gentle, controlled landing in the event of a failure. So, if things get eerily quiet, and your fuel consumption drops to zero, as a helicopter pilot you'll have better options on where to put the machine down. In this case Farmer Jake's bean field will do nicely.

Speaking of the maintenance aspect of either category, as airy-fairy as it sounds, I came to believe that helicopters have a personality, that each one, if treated well or ill, returns that sentiment to you. Taking care with the machinery will likely be much more important to you in a helicopter, simply for this reason.

The negative aspects of commercial helicopter operations aren't numerous, nor onerous, but they are noteworthy. For one thing, as a rotary-wing pilot you'll commonly work at the end of the road, especially when you're a rookie. On one of my first jobs, I was posted to the middle of Alaska, where hordes of skeeters often massed in sufficient numbers to kill young animals (true story), and bears dropped by my hut at all hours to scrounge for snacks (also true). My Alaskan post may not have been at the end of the earth, but I could see it from there. I needed the hours, so I took the job. The upside to taking such jobs is that they can often provide you more real-world experience than others do, for a richer, more memorable experience.

Another advantage to jobs in the bush is that you'll often be *The* pilot. That is, when you arrive at the job site, there's no need to look for a fellow pilot, because there ain't one. You're it. Being the sole operator of a helicopter day in and out gives you the opportunity to really know the machine's flight characteristics, its quirks, and its limitations. It also demands from you a thorough understanding of the maintenance aspects of flying the machine and keeping it FAA legal. In a later chapter, I discuss the benefits and drawbacks to you of holding licensure as both a pilot and an Airframe and Powerplant (A&P) mechanic.

Helicopter jobs do tend to be mundane, crude, and often remote. However, that aspect of it could be a plus for you. If your preference is for remote, out-of-the-way places, and exotic,

CHAPTER 5: ROTARY-WING?

arcane flying missions, there are likely more of those positions on the rotary-wing side of aviation. My hospital flying was an example. After twenty years of air medical flying I never experienced two duty shifts the same. Beyond that, with the exception of the power pole counting job I'll describe later, and a few times flying news and traffic when I could have phoned the information in, I never had a boring day of flying.

Commercial helicopter ops may offer you equipment that's barely airworthy, so the walkaround and preflight inspections you'll do are much more critical. Also, your missions may tend to be gritty and dissatisfying, your customers can be demanding and surly, paychecks can be meager, and owners/operators with sometimes egregious flight demands can put a lot of pressure on you when they know FAA's enforcement focus is on the airlines, not on them.

In much of the helicopter community, if you fly in remote areas, for example, forget crew rest regulations. They'll be lax at best, and pretty much unenforceable in the bush in any case. Especially as a first job, the clear message to you from an operator could be that if you don't fly the assigned trip, another pilot will. And if you accept a flight, and there's a subsequent FAA enforcement action, it will be on you. The operator can simply claim that you accepted the flight, and he'll be off the hook.

As for pay and bennies, I can only pass along to you what I once knew about it, as I've been retired for a while. When I left aviation, my last posting had been as a tour pilot on Kauai. The job was not salaried; I was paid per hop around the island. But in 2005, the last year I flew, I earned in the neighborhood of $75,000. Bear in mind the job was in Hawaii where paychecks must have bigger numbers due to the outlandish cost of living in the islands. When I was on Kauai, for example, a loaf of bread cost five bucks, and there were numerous other financial incentives to live elsewhere.

What I'm passing along to you is the somber, almost harsh side of helicopter aviation. After reading the above, you might well ask if rotary-wing flying is for you. However, what I said previously is also true. I couldn't imagine a better, more fulfilling life in the sky for myself than being at the controls of a helicopter. When I was a kid, I'd watched that Bell 47 pilot land and take off near my backyard, and the image and desire stuck with me. I decided that day that I wanted to be a pilot, and I eventually got my wish. I flew for fifty years, and I'd do it again in half a heartbeat.

There's something sublime about hovering. Bringing the collective pitch up, feeling the helicopter rouse itself, then defy gravity and lift from the ground is superbly gratifying. Regardless of which helicopter I flew, the two-seat Hughes 269, the Bell UH-1 Huey, the AS-350 AStar, on up to the 50,000 pound gross weight Boeing CH-47, the thrill of hovering never diminished. Holding 7,000 horsepower in my left hand on the thrust lever when flying a Chinook was an amazing feeling and an awesome responsibility. I recommend it to anyone who thinks flying helicopters is dull.

For twenty years I flew a medical helicopter for a hospital, far and away the best flying job I ever had. Helping sick and injured people went a long way toward explaining why I became a pilot in the first place. Flying tourists on Kauai was deeply gratifying as well, perhaps not quite so rewarding as air medical, but awfully close. The best part of flying tours, for me, was the chance to exhibit skills that very few people have, at the apex of my flying career. It was extremely satisfying to take nervous, white-knuckled passengers on a tour, and to see them relax and enjoy themselves within minutes of takeoff. Often my most fearful passengers on Kauai asked after landing if they could go up again! That was a great feeling.

Yet another reason for you to fly helicopters is the sheer thrill of it. Flying an airplane can reward you in many ways. It can offer you a degree of maneuverability and the visceral thrill of being airborne, but nothing provides you thrills like flying a helicopter does.

One reason for that is that helicopters are inherently

unstable machines. That sounds like a defect or a negative observation. It's not. It simply means that airplanes are inherently stable in the air, so they demand less attention from you to stay upright. Once airborne, at speed, at altitude, and trimmed up just right, if you don't interfere too much with an airplane it will fly itself for a long time. A helicopter will not. Period. Removing your hands from the controls of a helicopter is the surest way for you to prove the existence of gravity. Without an autopilot, a helicopter must be flown all the time. That realization offers you the benefit of knowing that your life is literally in your hands. You may find that disconcerting; I enjoyed it.

Another personal consideration is the vanity of being able to fly a helicopter, something very few people can do. I'm convinced that most pilots of either category, helicopter or fixed-wing, harbor a touch of exhibitionism. We're showoffs, I believe, just better paid, and with a larger audience than a standup comic. For me, an enjoyable part of flying tours was demonstrating my skill at handling the aircraft, especially when a passenger would comment on how smooth the flight had gone.

So, I'm happy I chose to fly helicopters. My rich Uncle Sam paid for my training. He even gave me a year-long assignment for a bit of on-the-job training, all expenses paid, and that helped with the decision as well. But rotary-wing was the absolute best career choice for me. In the next chapter,

CHAPTER 5: ROTARY-WING?

I discuss the transition I made from military aviation to the civilian, commercial world and how difficult that journey can be for you.

One last note: Do you really want to fly? Or do you want others to see you as a pilot? We sometimes pursue things, including career goals, because we imagine how other people view us. This is certainly true in aviation. Being honest with yourself is a good start in addressing this issue.

Lessons:
- Single pilot or flying with company: It's a choice.
- Rookie jobs in either category can be dirty, depressing, and dangerous.
- Corporate aviation is lucrative, clean, and often boring.
- Imagine yourself in both cockpits and ask why you chose to fly.
- Do you want to fly? Or do you want others to see you flying?

—An old pilot

Chapter 6
TRANSITION:
Military to Commercial

At Hunter Army Airfield, February 1970

I'd fly a Huey today if they'd let me.

—*An old pilot*

A question I heard occasionally in my career was, "How do I become a pilot?" My default response was always, "Join the military." The Army, for example, often needs pilots, and if you can pass the flight aptitude test, and a flight physical, and then get through flight school, they'll teach you to fly helicopters and pay you for your trouble. You may not pile hours in a logbook in the Army, but then you just might.

In any case, joining the military for flight training is what I've always recommended[10].

Another thing to remember is that someday you may wish to retire. After serving in the active military, joining the National Guard or Reserve is an option, and the Guard on occasion has open slots for flight school. You can fly for a Guard or Reserve outfit, build hours, and continue with the same unit after landing a commercial flying job. This is the route I took. I flew only two years on active military duty, then twenty-eight more in the National Guard. For eighteen of those NG years, I flew both commercially and in the Guard.

Civilian employers are much better attuned to your need for time off during Guard activity these days, so leaving work for military obligations is (relatively) easy. Also, Guard units commonly have members who are commercial pilots, so firsthand knowledge of job openings can be just a drill weekend away for you.

CHAPTER 6: TRANSITION: MILITARY TO COMMERCIAL

Some of the benefits of flying in the Guard are the extra compensation, retirement points, building flight hours, filling a need for the community, and the simple camaraderie that goes along with serving your community. Additionally, Guard aviation helps with proficiency. It can also give you, as a helicopter pilot, the opportunity to practice instrument flying skills, something you're not likely to get in the civilian helicopter world. Lastly, depending on what equipment your Guard unit has, the National Guard can offer access to flight simulators in which you can practice emergency scenarios that can't be duplicated in the aircraft.

Going the military route has its potential perils for you, of course. You could end up on foreign soil in some bad guy's crosshairs, but the chances of that are remote, and if the enemy dude pokes holes in your aircraft the government will understand. They might even give you a medal or two. I received a few attaboy medals, though they didn't enhance my commercial résumé one little bit. Plus, if your flying machine gets shot full of holes the friendly unit wrench-bender will fix them. Many commercial helicopter pilots logged their first flight hours in military machines with the intention of moving to the commercial side later on.

A word of caution about flying with the military: You may indeed be deployed to a war zone and going to war is not a day at the beach, I can tell you. War will change you in ways you never wanted, nor expected. If you fly in combat, you may not like the person in the mirror as much as you once did. War changes anyone it touches, and not often in a good way. In my previous book, *A Vietnam Anthem, What the War Gave Me*, I explore this theme in detail, based on my year of flying in Vietnam. It was far beyond flight school; it was life school, and at times I wasn't sure I passed.

If you favor civilian training, either a Part 61 or Part 141 flight school, there are a number to choose from, and again depending on the category of aircraft you choose to fly—either rotary-wing, or fixed-wing—there's a school to cater to your needs. A civilian school was not my experience, so my knowledge of that is limited. But from what I hear those schools can be sufficiently attuned to a student's needs that you'll learn to fly, and that's a start. Some schools offer limited employment opportunities following graduation, either as an instructor with the school itself once certifications are earned, or with various aviation companies.

Costs of civilian schools appear to be similar across the board. Do your homework, read testimonials, talk to recent graduates, buy them a beer, and in general keep your eyes open. One thing to check would be the school's maintenance capability and track record. The better an aircraft looks, the better it flies.

CHAPTER 6: TRANSITION: MILITARY TO COMMERCIAL

It's a homely old truism, but it contains a bit of wisdom.

Unless you have a wealthy parent or relation willing to get their checkbook out for you, it's not feasible to just buy your way into aviation, and that's a good thing. The existing pay-your-own-way arrangement highlights capacity and merit, instead of simple financial status.

As to the choice between a Part 141 training school, and a Part 61 school, there are advantages to both.[11] It depends on several factors such as proximity to your home, pace of learning, category you wish to fly, costs, employment opportunities for you, and the quality of instruction.

One advantage of a Part 141 flight school is that you can progress more quickly, thus you gain certifications with fewer hours in the aircraft. While a private certificate requires you to log forty flight hours under Part 61, you'll be required to fly only thirty-five hours under Part 141. You can obtain a commercial certificate in just 190 flight hours at a Part 141 school, as opposed to 250 hours under Part 61.

Part 141 schools must have satisfactory performance/graduation rates. And because the FAA doesn't check on them quite as frequently, Part 61 schools and instructors aren't always penalized for being sub-par. A high failure rate at a Part 61 school may go unnoticed, and students could be squeezed for more money as a result, though any school worth a nickel would avoid that reputation. In a Part 141 school, sub-par instruction is subject to review by the FAA to ensure a proper training environment.

As for student loans toward flight school, you can purchase a package deal offering a block of flight hours at a discounted price rather than a pay-as-you-go plan. Paying up front, while appearing risky, can force you to fly more often, both to get your money's worth, and to have better retention of what you've learned. Sobering as it may be, final flight training costs can be way off. This is probably less likely at a Part 141 school, because their curricula are subject to more oversight.

However, the bottom line should not be the bottom line. If you can't imagine another career, and being a pilot is something you simply must do, go for it.

Here are some tips for making your move between military and commercial cockpits and reasons why that can be so damned hard. There's a whole lot more to it than swapping outfits. The transition is a difficult process for every pilot I've encountered. It was certainly a speed bump for me, even though, when I started flying commercially, I'd flown in the active military for just two years. For a twenty-year retired military pilot the adjustment could be overwhelming.

One of the biggest changes for me when I transitioned to

CHAPTER 6: TRANSITION: MILITARY TO COMMERCIAL

commercial aviation was becoming cost conscious. In the Army I never gave the price of fuel, parts, maintenance, insurance, or staff salary a passing nod. I thought overhead was where the circuit breakers were.

Unconcerned with the cost per flight hour of operating a Huey, for example, I just hopped into the cockpit, fired up the engine, and took off. If a system or part had spit up during a flight, I'd scribble an entry in the log, and usually that very night it would be repaired. The military mentality is, "let taxpayers foot the bill; they're good at it." In the real world, where people like taxpayers must be aware of costs, it's a different matter.

After flying in the Army, I was used to having a co-pilot. Even though, as I mentioned in a previous chapter, I preferred flying by myself. When I stepped into a commercial cockpit all alone the first time it was jarring. I had to be sure the machine was airworthy, since there was no crew chief in attendance. I had to study the logbook to make sure paperwork was in order and that any FAA restrictions, such as airworthiness directives (ADs) or service bulletins (SBs), had been addressed, something a military pilot never does, because the ship's mechanic takes care of that.

I had to observe simple things that would keep me safe. For one minor example, in nearly every setting I encountered in commercial flying the red sock method was used as a warning signal. If I found a red sock draped over the cyclic, it wasn't there to keep the stick warm, it told me the aircraft wasn't flyable for some reason.

Something that will affect you in both civilian and military aircraft is collective care of the equipment. No one wants to fly a machine that's been rode hard and put to bed wet. In other words, no conscientious pilot wants to step into the cockpit of a wrung-out aircraft after a careless colleague lands it. The concept should be reality in the military, too, but it's especially relevant in the commercial world where not only will you be earning a living with a tool that just happens to be an aircraft, but paying passengers rely on the integrity of the machine to get where they're going and, with any luck, still alive when they get there.

I never liked cowboy pilots, the showoffs who take aircraft to the limits and beyond for their own thrills. Those pilots should be drummed out of the business. Here's a lesson: It's easy to get wrapped up in the thrill of flying and overlook the fact that...you're a pilot. In other words, it's easy to forget that you're defying gravity while you're cruising across the sky. One of the most important lessons is that gravity isn't just a good idea; it's the law.

I'll tell you about one of the more sensitive topics in aviation: Your relationship with other pilots. For the most part, the colleagues I flew with were highly professional women and

CHAPTER 6: TRANSITION: MILITARY TO COMMERCIAL

men. Both in the military and commercially, most of them were conscientious, capable, dedicated people who had the same desire I did: to have a long and prosperous flying career, and then die at home in my sleep. But there were a few pilots I met who didn't meet the exacting standards I expected, and their behavior stood out for the contrast. These "cowboys" give aviation a bad name by disregarding rules and overstressing aircraft.

A fellow named Jim B comes to mind. Jim was a young guy without much experience when he came aboard with the tour operator I flew for on Kauai. He was killed in a Helicopter EMS crash in California several years ago.

Jim got sideways with our boss at Air Kauai for his questionable flying. In the first weeks he flew tours, Jim frightened a few of his customers. Once he nearly ran out of gas because he'd failed to refuel the helicopter after a tour and then took off on another one!

The question arises: When do you have an obligation to speak up? How soon do you intervene when you see a fellow pilot doing something that imperils them, or the mission, or the aircraft? When do you go beyond the sacred Pilot in Command wall of protection and speak out about behaviors that may harm or kill someone? It's not an easy thing, and it's rarely done, even in the strictest aviation environments.

Jim B left Kauai in 2005 when the boss had finally received

enough negative reports from his passengers and fired him. He took a job with an air medical operation in California. In November 2009, he crashed near Reno, Nevada killing himself and two medical personnel. Jim was a marginal pilot. I knew it. Why didn't I speak up? Had I called out his cavalier attitude and mentioned his unprofessional flying, he might still be alive and the medical crew who died with him might be as well. Humility can be a negative attribute.

At some point as a pilot, you'll have a duty to police your own ranks. I'm afraid it happens very seldom, and the aviation industry suffers for this lack of accountability. This is especially true in the helicopter side of commercial flying, partly because aircraft are typically flown single-pilot, eliminating the possibility of direct observation of pilot behaviors and skills.

There are more challenges in transitioning from military to commercial flying. Using the comm radios is different, for example. You may be conversant with ATC communication procedures, but as a commercial pilot if you miss a radio call, botch a clearance, bust your airspace, or commit a violation of FARs, the stakes can be higher for you than for a military pilot. While using the national airspace system, military pilots fly with a layer of protection. I'm not aware of any military pilot receiving an FAA violation for a transgression.

As the sole pilot, you'll have to attend to simple things like

CHAPTER 6: TRANSITION: MILITARY TO COMMERCIAL

'remove-before-flight' flags, the aircraft's weight and balance, seeing that passengers receive an adequate safety briefing, and that their needs are met. You must make sure needed charts or other navigation documents are on board and current. Very few of those items are the sole responsibility of a military pilot, since flying in the military is typically a crew endeavor, and much of the peripheral stuff can be delegated.

As for the crew concept, in my case it wasn't just that I'd been used to flying with another pilot across the cockpit; I was accustomed to flying *as a crew*. In the military, you always fly with at least two crewmembers in the aircraft, very often three, and sometimes more. So, strapping into the aircraft by yourself, and handling every aspect of a flight, takes some getting used to. I enjoyed solo flying very much but doing so was a strange feeling the first few times.

Another difficult transition into commercial aviation, for me, was recognizing the alien concept of a visual flight rules (VFR)-only aircraft. With the exception of the OH-58 observation helicopter, the Army version of the Bell 206 Jet Ranger, every aircraft I flew in the military had instrument flight rules (IFR) equipment on board. In commercial aviation I flew seventeen different types of helicopters, and only two of them were IFR equipped. So, transitioning to a VFR-only machine affected every weather decision I made. Because of this, I developed more awareness of changing weather patterns and potential dangers, and I was more cautious about accepting assignments. The backside of it was that, in the commercial flying world, especially flying a helicopter in EMS, the pressure to fly often *increased* with worsening weather, so my go/no-go decisions often had more import, when a critical patient awaited the helicopter's arrival.

After transitioning to commercial flying, you must cater to civilian passengers, possibly for the first time. Flying military machines, all of which are built as tactical vehicles, with no consideration for passenger comfort, there are no onboard luxuries. Hauling troops was a get in, buckle up, hold on, and no whining affair. My 'passengers' in the Army would have been offended had I pampered them. In the commercial world they'd have been offended if I didn't.

One thing I missed about military flying was the camaraderie offered in a group of fellow aviators, especially after long, grueling, possibly perilous missions. In the military, dangerous operations are the stock in trade. In civilian flying, not so much. While carrying civilians your primary goal will be an uneventful flight. If my commercial passengers fell asleep, that was a mark of success. If troops fell asleep in the back of the Chinook, we figured we had a gas leak.

The biggest obstacle you may face while transitioning is

CHAPTER 6: TRANSITION: MILITARY TO COMMERCIAL

the fact that you may have to pay dues all over again. Accepting a starting position in commercial aviation can mean less status, and possibly a smaller paycheck. The commercial flying community, especially in helicopters, is surprisingly small. I learned not to piss somebody off, because that person likely knew someone, who knew someone else, etc. Sometimes only two or three degrees of separation will exist between you and that other pilot, so learn to make nice, and that will give your career a better chance to thrive.

Paying dues again may be very difficult for you if you've been in the military many years. If you leave the military with an exalted rank, a cap slathered with egg salad, with lots of flight time, the highest aviator badges, and a hefty paycheck, it may not be easy to start at the bottom. It depends on how badly you want the job, I suppose.

Another more nuanced aspect of that scenario is that military pilots tend to be sticklers for the rules and regulations. I won't say that the commercial world is nonchalant about such things, but absolute, strict, unbending adherence to regulations, especially if that adherence is vocal, has marked many a military-trained commercial pilot, and not in a good way. A colleague I flew with at the hospital many years ago was shown the door concerning a weather call. Charles spouted FAA ceiling and visibility regs by the numbers. The flight nurses had a patient to tend to. Both parties were right in that case, but it didn't matter. The flight nurses wanted a simple yes or no; Charles gave them chapter and verse. He was gone shortly afterward.

One of my first aviation jobs taught me about differences between military and commercial flying the hard way. Indeed, it was the first time in my life I got fired.

In 1981, I accepted a position in Toledo Ohio with a brand new charter helicopter service titled Fly By Helicopter Inc. A local real estate poo-bah had purchased a Bell 206L-1 LongRanger. He hired me to fly it, and appointed a fellow named Don K to oversee the start-up charter business.

Well, the business side and the aviation side squabbled right away. Don and I had major differences on how to promote the business: I wanted to put potential clients' butts in the seats and take them flying. Don wanted to put those same butts in seats in meeting rooms and do 'death by PowerPoint.' Long story short, Don and I decided we'd get along a lot better if we parted ways. So, with two weeks' severance pay in my pocket, I put Toledo Ohio in the rearview mirror, and went seeking a new position.

I was fortunate to find a new job right away with a contractor in Indiana. A stipulation in the fellow's insurance policy for the helicopter stated that any potential pilot must have had the manufacturer's school for the aircraft. The Toledo

CHAPTER 6: TRANSITION: MILITARY TO COMMERCIAL

operation had sent me to that school at Bell Helicopter, since pilot training was included with every new helicopter purchase. So, the The Fly By Helicopter adventure had qualified me, albeit inadvertently, for the Evansville job. Indeed, the Toledo detour was filled with lessons that I'll itemize ending this chapter.

Just like isobars on weather charts, an aviation life has very few straight lines.

First flying jobs, especially in helicopters, may take you to the end of the road. Some may take you where there *is* no road. I worked a few of those rough, challenging jobs miles away from civilization and some were humbling. But they put hours in my logbook, and more importantly they exposed me to other pilots and other positions. Simply hearing about a job can often be your vector into it. However, if a flying job has been advertised, and no one has taken it, it may be a position you don't want.

As for seeking a commercial job, another route for you is, of course, to find an instructor's seat. This applies to both fixed and rotary-wing. The best way for you to learn something is to teach it to others. There are other paths to employment in aviation but signing on with a Part 141 school as an instructor can be an efficient way to find decent employment. You may find that you really enjoy flight instruction and do it for a long time.

My way to the cockpit was through a year in Vietnam, and then by flying in the National Guard. I had a colleague in my Guard unit who was a Bell Helicopter salesman. Steve knew who was buying the aircraft. His job was to facilitate those transactions. So, anyone in that Guard unit looking for a flying job made nice with Steve. My first position came through his connections. Steve had closed the deal for the LongRanger with Fly By Helicopter in Toledo. So, look for an aircraft salesperson, buy them a bottle of something stronger than Diet Pepsi and you may find a job.

Note: On a few of my remote assignments, I met pilots who also had an Airframe and Powerplant (A&P) license, that is, certification as mechanics. Those pilots had a leg up when seeking employment with companies working remotely, because they could both fly and fix the aircraft, thus saving the company money. This extra certification is something to consider, however it was also my experience that individuals with both tickets were rarely compensated for the time and expense they'd devoted to obtaining the A&P license. They may have been hired more readily, but their paychecks were no different.

CHAPTER 6: TRANSITION: MILITARY TO COMMERCIAL

Lessons:
- Military flight school can expedite your career.
- A part 61 school may be cheaper but a 141 school may be better.
- Choosing a category is critical. FW or RW? Both have pluses and minuses.
- If/when a company sells the aircraft you've been flying, put copies of your resumé somewhere inside it. The buyer may need a pilot.
- If you learn of an upcoming flying slot and you don't want it for yourself, pass the information along to a fellow aviator. The gesture could repay you along the way.
- Crossing from military to commercial will be difficult. You'll adapt, but don't expect the two scenarios to be the same.
- Ref: my Toledo job, here are the lessons:
    1. A helicopter charter business will never work.
    2. Businesspeople think differently than pilots.
    3. Getting fired can be a great career boost.

—An old pilot

Chapter 7

STRETCHING THE RULES

AS-350 B-2 AStar/H-125

Part of learning to fly is unlearning preconceptions.

—*An old pilot*

I would never encourage you, especially if you're a rookie, to break the rules. An old aviation adage says that rules and regulations are written in blood, so if you take the rules lightly, ignore them, don't know them, or otherwise dismiss the rules as irrelevant you'll eventually pay. So, follow the rules.

You may be faced with an emergency sometime in your career that demands an entirely different approach to flying. You may lose an engine on takeoff or collect a load of ice and be going down, or have vital equipment fail at the worst possible time. Your emergency checklist will likely address these situations of course, so always know your emergency procedures, and that should keep you safe.

But there's another element to emergencies that can't be taught. It can only be learned, and that is acting beyond what's written in the checklist. If you've done all the appropriate emergency procedures and you're still in danger, don't be afraid to do whatever you feel may work to save yourself and your aircraft. In a 1954 movie titled *The High and The Mighty*, two pilots are flying between Hawaii and California when one of the two engines on the plane loses power. They have a long way yet to fly, and very different styles of addressing the emergency. The younger pilot, who happens to be the captain, decides to ditch in the ocean, in other words to give up.

The older, more experienced pilot, who happens to be the

CHAPTER 7: STRETCHING THE RULES

co-pilot, demands that they keep flying. The two men argue over which course of action to take. Finally, the older pilot convinces the captain to do whatever it takes to get to the coast. In the end, the plane lands safely, but only after extraordinary measures to save it. The lesson is to do whatever works, even if it's not written in a checklist.

Here's a personal war story from a time I stretched the rules to accomplish a mission in Vietnam. Events like these will (hopefully) be rare in your aviation career. Keep in mind that I was receiving small arms fire at the time this happened, and I simply had no choice but to do what I describe here.

In September 1970, I was Pilot in Command of the second Huey in a flight of four on a mission to rescue a small recon team in Laos. The ground troops were under fire, and needed to be evacuated, so our flight of Hueys launched to pick them up.[12]

The pickup zone was on a steep hillside, so I was unable to land. Each aircraft had been fitted with a coiled aluminum ladder that could be dropped over the right side of the cargo bay, allowing men on the landing zone (LZ) to climb up into the helicopter. Our flight of four Hueys arrived over the location, and the flight lead started in.

From my view as the second aircraft, I watched the lead Huey descend then I slowed down and waited my turn. I soon realized that I was crowding him, so I did a quick pedal turn to the left, and then lined back up. But when I turned around, the lead Huey was on its side on the LZ, its rotor blades twisted like pretzels, and jet fuel seeping down the hill. He'd been shot down!

I raced to the LZ, stopped at a hover, and told my crew to drop our ladder, which quickly clunked out the right side of the aircraft. Shortly, the flight crew of the destroyed helicopter hustled up into my Huey. One after another they appeared, gathering on the cabin floor behind me. I held the hover, while hearing the snap and pop of AK-47 rounds at my left, and with the stink of spilled jet fuel filling my nostrils.

With flight lead's crew aboard, I attempted to take off. I eased the cyclic forward, with the torque gauge bumping up against its red line limit of fifty pounds. Beyond that limit, rotor RPM would likely decay, making the takeoff more difficult.

Hovering demands the highest amount of engine power. As a helicopter moves forward to take off, it moves through its own downwash into clean air, a passage called translational lift. Going through this phase of flight the aircraft will lose a bit of altitude, until it meets clean air and power demand drops. I had no altitude to spare. I had no power to spare, either.

Fighting to take off, I coaxed the Huey forward toward clean air, as the torque gauge climbed even higher. The gauge soon read fifty-two pounds, and my rotor RPM began to sag.

CHAPTER 7: STRETCHING THE RULES

In the next several minutes I learned what kind of pilot I was, and what I did that day to address the situation required me to stretch the rules.

Another aspect of helicopter operations is this: At a hover, the tail rotor keeps the aircraft lined up in the direction the pilot wants. But it also uses 15% of available engine power.

At the time, I was holding the left pedal almost fully forward, using all of the tail rotor's pitch to keep the nose of the aircraft lined up. The pedal bumped against the stop at times, just to keep the nose straight. Then I thought, why am I doing that? I didn't need to line up with anything, I needed to get those men out of there. My alignment wouldn't matter a hoot if I went down, except perhaps to create a more graceful crash sequence, and nobody cared about that.

If I released the pedal, two things would happen: The Huey's nose would yaw to the right, giving the engine more power, which would give me more RPM. I might have gained the power I needed to take off!

I relaxed the left pedal, and as I knew it would, the nose of the helicopter yawed wildly right. Then the torque needle dropped below fifty pounds, and RPM recovered. I eased the cyclic forward a bit more, went through translational lift into clean, undisturbed air, and took off.

I had stretched the rules and salvaged the operation. I

could hear Wayne Alexander screaming at me: *"Trim!, RPM!, Power!"* But I knew he'd approve what I'd done as well, and that he'd spare me the yellow pencil treatment for once.

> **Stretching the rules requires a damn good rationale. Saving your aircraft and passengers is the only one that makes sense.**
> —*An old pilot*

My war story has another element to it, one that seems counterintuitive. Sometimes in the rush to remedy a problem, you'll have the impulse to flip switches, or you'll rush to fix a malfunction, just to do something! But be careful. By acting quickly, you can hurt yourself. A recent helicopter emergency medical services (HEMS) aircraft crashed in North Carolina when, instead of identifying an engine that was losing power, the pilot shut down the good engine, a recurring problem in multi-engine aircraft, both fixed and rotary-wing. The extra time it takes to assess and confirm what's really happening can save your life, so slow down, and figure out what the real emergency is. Don't make it worse or create a new one.

There are times when you must perform emergency procedures as quickly as possible. But you're often better served by slowing down, discerning what the problem really is, and how you must address it. Here's an example:

CHAPTER 7: STRETCHING THE RULES

I was in the left seat of a Chinook cargo helicopter one afternoon flying 3,000 feet above Lake Superior. I had a ten-ton load hanging under the helicopter on two cables. One cable was attached to the front cargo hook, the other to the rear one. Suddenly, on the caution panel, the "Hook Open" light flashed on. Instantly, out of instinct, I raised my hand overhead to the load release switch. I was prepared to pickle the load into the water to save the aircraft. If that load had broken free of just one cargo hook, it would have swung loose, and dragged the aircraft down with it.

My right-seater saw my hand go up to the pickle switch. "Are you sure you want to do that?" he said.

I wasn't at all sure I wanted to do that, so I waited. We were still flying straight and level. The gauges were within range. The only difference from before was that the "Hook Open" light was glowing on the panel. I asked for the crew's input. *"Load's steady,"* they said. So, I took my hand off the pickle switch, and started breathing again. If I'd released the load, it would have dropped into Lake Superior, demanding enough paperwork to match the load's weight. As it turned out, a lone microswitch on the offending cargo hook was simply out of adjustment, which is why the light blinked on. I had waited, assessed, and kept flying, and I'm glad I did.

During your career you will see other pilots disregard regulations, flying in a way that you know is either dangerous, or careless. You'll watch these colleagues do things they shouldn't do, ignoring rules that have been crafted for a very good reason, and performing in a way that makes you question their professionalism. It will be very difficult, maybe impossible, to confront them, especially if these pilots are in a position of authority with you. Here's an example from my years of flying tours in Hawaii and how other pilots' casual disregard of rules can cause tension and confrontation.

The helicopter tour business on Kauai was intensely competitive. When I flew on the island there were seven operators, each one competing not only for customers, but to catch their competitor's pilots breaking the rules to bring the FAA into the squabble.

There were a lot of rules in tour flying. Due to the number of tour helicopter accidents in Hawaii, and the fatalities they've caused through the years, the FAA watches every move tour operators and pilots make, and they cite any infractions. Typically, those punitive measures result from weather violations, ignoring terrain proximity rules, or overwater operations too far from shore. When I flew on Kauai under Part 135 of the Federal Air Regulations, the rule stated that a single-engine tour helicopter may be flown offshore only within power-off gliding

CHAPTER 7: STRETCHING THE RULES

distance to land. Other regulations dictated how close to terrain features we were authorized to go and still others cited weather minimums and required passenger flotation equipment.

I'd been flying commercially at the time for thirty years, and when I saw my colleagues at other tour companies breaking the rules, which some pilots did on a regular basis, I was torn. Do I report them to the FAA in hopes that they'll change their behavior and fly more professionally? Do I look the other way and hope they don't have an engine failure offshore or fly into a mountain in low visibility? It was a dilemma I quite frankly never resolved for myself.

After I retired from flying, I noticed that the rules had changed. Solely affecting tour helicopter operators, a new Part 136 entered the FAA books. This new set of regulations was effective in 2008 and sought to curtail further tour helicopter accidents.

To summarize, don't be hesitant to stretch rules if you find yourself in a safety of flight situation, and without alternatives. Remember, you'll be the pilot in command of the aircraft and according to the regulations whatever decision you make is yours alone. This responsibility is not conveyed quickly or to just anyone; it must be earned and protected. As a colleague says, any decision made for convenience is likely the wrong one. So preflight the aircraft well, know your EPs, take your time if something goes wrong, and remember, your biggest job-always, is to fly the aircraft.

Lessons:
- Stretch the rules only with a damn good reason. Saving your aircraft and passengers is about the only one.
- Keep your head on a swivel, always.
- It doesn't have to look pretty, just safe.
- Emergency? Slow down; it could save your life.
- Always fly first. Remember: Aviate, Navigate, Communicate.

—An old pilot

Chapter 8
SA: SITUATIONAL AWARENESS

Cessna 177 Cardinal
Beautiful, pilot-friendly airplane

With experience, you'll develop a sixth sense, an inner alarm that chimes when something either inside or outside the cockpit isn't quite right. Either another aircraft's position and route of flight poses a potential threat, an odd gauge reading catches your eye, or a crew member says something that sounds out of place and potentially alarming to you. You'll sit up straighter and pay attention.

Here's an example. One dim yet flyable night in Iowa, when I was halfway to a rural hospital, the flight nurse opened her intercom, "Sure is a JFK junior kind of night, isn't it?" It was a few months after John F. Kennedy junior had been killed in a crash involving marginal weather. The flight nurse was hinting to me that the weather was similar, and she was nervous. What she should have said was, *"I'm not comfortable, can we turn around?"*

Hearing what she *didn't* say, I canceled the flight, and returned to base. The addendum to this event was a renewed emphasis among the crew that there's no shame in speaking up. Another pilot may have ignored the flight nurse's comment about the weather and continued on. Our crews had a policy that said three to go, one to say no, and that's why I aborted the mission.

With more hours accrued in the cockpit, your sense of situational awareness (SA), the little voice in your head that says something's amiss will get sharper, until you'll be able to project

CHAPTER 8: SA: SITUATIONAL AWARENESS

ahead of the aircraft. This ability will become one of the better items in your toolbox. Some pilot's refer to it as air sense.

The other side of this perceptive ability, however, is its scarcity in newer, younger pilots, simply because of a lack of experience. You'll often dismiss a feeling of unease, or a sense that something's not quite right because you're a rookie. Veteran pilots may dismiss your fears as well. It shouldn't happen, but it does. My advice is to listen to your little voice; it can keep you alive.

Once, when I was a fairly inexperienced pilot in Vietnam, I noticed a discoloration on the helicopter engine's burner can and asked an older maintenance fellow to take a look at it. He looked it over, then he berated me for disturbing him and told me not to worry about the mark, insinuating that I was just afraid to fly. I went over his head, and his superior supported my concern. I can still hear the exchange between the two men: "This aircraft will fly just fine," the first one said. "Yep, for about ten minutes," said the other. I felt vindicated, of course. Despite the older fellow's grumbling, I got the issue addressed and flew another day.

Here are a few more times that my sixth sense kicked in, telling me that something wasn't as it should be.

I took off from the hospital one afternoon and flew just a

few miles when I noticed the torque gauge needle acting weird. It jumped a bit, did a little whifferdill dance, dropped down the gauge, jumped back up, and then did the act all over again. I didn't like what I was seeing, so I aborted the mission, returned to the helipad, and landed.

The torque measuring system in the AStar helicopter (once labeled the AS350, now called an Airbus H-125) uses a wet gauge. From the torque metering system on the engine, oil is routed directly into the gauge to give a real time reading. So, I suspected the oil level. Sure enough, when I removed the reservoir cap and checked the fluid level, there was perhaps a cup or two of liquid in the tank, when the full level should have been eight quarts. The reservoir was white plastic. The mechanic filled it to the same level each day and as he did, over time, a discoloration of the plastic appeared to *be* the actual oil level. When I'd done a preflight that day, in haste I glanced at the reservoir, saw the stain, and felt satisfied that the oil level was sufficient.

My sixth sense while watching the torque needle was self-generated. Afterward, I learned to look inside the oil can to make sure what I was seeing was oil. A side note to this incident: I posted a report to the company about it, and they passed my concern about the plastic tank along to the manufacturer. Later versions of the AStar came with a metal oil tank complete with

CHAPTER 8: SA: SITUATIONAL AWARENESS

a sight gauge window. It's likely I had nothing to do with the change, but it was good to see it anyway. Sometimes we must be our own advocates for safe operations. Engineers and designers are nice folks, but they're only going to fall off an eighteen-inch chair.

I was assigned a mission to resupply a unit on the ground near Khe Sanh. It was early in the monsoon season in Vietnam. The weather was crappy, chilly, windy, and variable. With my crew aboard, I pointed the Huey toward the Khe Sanh plain, and started over the mountains. Halfway across the range we encountered severe turbulence and lowering visibility. Weather was changing fast enough, and the turbulence was banging the helicopter around so badly that it was hard to fly. I knew my crew was nervous because the intercom stayed silent. Neither of the three men with me said a word. As the weather worsened, I knew as aircraft commander that it was my call to continue the mission or not.

The ground troops needed their beans and bullets, but I wasn't going to sacrifice my crew to get supplies to them. The resupply could wait a while. I called the ground commander, told him we weren't coming that day, and turned around. The intercom opened up right away. "Good decision, sir," my crew chief said. "I agree," my right-seater echoed his opinion.

We went home, tied the blades down, and called it a day. I

caught a minimal amount of flack for calling the mission off, but that didn't faze me. The safety of my crew was my priority.

Later that day, I learned that a helicopter from another company had gone down in the same location where I'd turned around. They were trying to get to Khe Sanh and crashed in the mountains. It took a rescue team two days to find the aircraft. There were no survivors.

The same scenario played out a few years later. In the summer of 1980, I took a job in Panama to fly from a tuna boat as a spotter. I'd be flying a Bell 47 on floats, taking off from the small boat to circle overhead looking for schools of fish. But as soon as I arrived at the hangar in Panama City my alarm bells started clanging. The aircraft was in dozens of pieces on the hangar floor. Men milled around smoking cigarettes, littering the floor with soda cans and trash, and taking their time on every task.

The biggest concern I had centered on the tail rotor assembly. One of the mechanics explained that the wear pattern on the gearbox wasn't typical, that the gears appeared to be clashing in such a way that if the problem wasn't corrected the gearbox might rupture. Slightly alarmed, but glad he was on top of the issue, I waited for the aircraft to be reassembled so I could fly it onto the boat and get to work.

That was a Thursday. I only know that because I'd been

CHAPTER 8: SA: SITUATIONAL AWARENESS

to the boat and met the crew. They were Portuguese men and during my introduction I'd told the captain about the issue with the helicopter. He told me to relax about it and mentioned something that I wasn't aware of. He said, "You have till at least Saturday. Portuguese crews never leave port on Friday. It's bad luck."

So, I returned to the hangar to oversee the assembly of the helicopter. What I saw there, and what set off my alarm again, convinced me to quit the job and go home. When I returned to the hangar after only a few hours, the same mechanic had reinstalled the tail rotor gearbox, and the rotor itself was mounted on it. "All fixed, good as new," he said, grinning, but not making eye contact. Two hours before that he'd been at a loss to explain the problem. Suddenly he'd identified it and fixed it?

I envisioned taking off from the boat, looking at all that really deep water, then having the gearbox come apart sending me diving into the blue Pacific. The risk wasn't worth taking. I called the company and quit, then caught a flight home to Ohio. Months later I heard that the pilot who'd replaced me went down in that aircraft, and the machine was lost at sea.

The lesson is clear. Had I ignored those warning signs and taken the job, that pilot would have been me. At the time I was only a few years out of the military. I needed the job, the money, and the experience. I quit the job anyway. If your senses warn you that something's amiss, you should heed them. It's too easy to grab onto a job just to fly or to fill your logbook.

Lessons:
- SA, Situational Awareness is a real thing—Trust it, use it.
- If your gut says something's wrong, something's wrong.
- Aircraft don't magically fix themselves.
- Regardless of how good a flying job looks, sometimes it's advisable to walk away.
- You're not flying for a paycheck; you're flying to build a legacy.
- Risk can never be zero; but it can be minimized.
- It's better to arrive late in this world, than early in the next.
- If it's bad on the ground, it will only get worse in the air.
- The law of gravity is not a general rule.

—An old pilot

Chapter 9
HIGH POINTS

Lockheed L-1049 Super Constellation

30 minutes in the left seat of this airplane gave me a lot of respect for pilots who crossed oceans in them.

—*An old pilot*

In this chapter I diverge from the technical, mechanical, hardware-heavy issues and tell you about a few of the high points of my own flying career. Not to get all airy-fairy about it but flying can put you in closer touch with some ineffable, often spiritual, side of living. Aviation is not a celebration of the mundane, or the prosaic. It leans more toward poetry.

As a new or potential pilot, you already appreciate this, or your dream to fly would never have germinated. Here are a few of the in-flight events I'll recall till my ultimate final approach and landing.

One of the high points of my career was being at the controls of an aircraft I was hopelessly unqualified to fly. The picture above of the Lockheed L-1049 Super Constellation is that aircraft. In the summer of 1997, following an airshow in Iowa City, I shelled out a donation to the Save A Connie foundation. The few bucks I donated secured me a seat in the cockpit for a short time, as the plane and its crew flew to Sioux City Iowa for the next show. Halfway to Sioux City, the captain escorted me to the front office of the big legendary Lockheed. I settled into the left seat and attempted to fly the big bird.

I say I *attempted* to fly it because, number one, I had at most seventy-five hours in a fixed-wing airplane of any kind at the time, all of it single-engine. Number two, I was quite frankly amazed at how heavy the plane's controls were. There was no autopilot. That particular airplane had been delivered brand new to a company called Slick Airways in 1959, in other words, long before *George* (a common term for the autopilot) would have been available for duty. I did have a co-pilot, and between the two of us, we wrestled the big Connie through the up and downdrafts of the hot Iowa sky.

It was a revelation to me how simple crosscurrents and turbulence pushed us around. We even had to adjust the controls for the movement of people in the cabin behind us as they walked around, going to the lavatory etc. It made me appreciate the intrepid, and likely wearied aviators who muscled those big planes across entire oceans. But it was fun to fly the Connie, a real aviation high point, nonetheless, and a particular thrill to see the crusty old pilot in command change seats with me and take over control of the big Lockheed like he'd been born in that seat.

In the summer of 1980, I was posted to the interior of Alaska on a firefighting contract. The equipment I flew, a Bell 205, was the civilian version of an Army Huey. I was using a Bambi Bucket®[13] slung under the aircraft to douse forest fires. It was an interesting summer, a bit wet, thus offering minimal firefighting activity, and not as much flight time as I'd hoped. But it offered the chance to fly, to practice killing steroidal skeeters, and to see some of the astonishing natural beauty of Alaska. It also stamped my logbook with an endorsement authorizing me to "herd bears by helicopter," a distinction few pilots have. Here's a short version of that war story:

He (she? The bear) was interfering with a firefighting crew I'd dropped off, and when Mr. Bear wouldn't allow them to put out the fire, they called me to come back and fetch them, or to move the bear out of their way. (Bears in Alaska are very smart. If they see smoke, they go toward it, because they know there'll be a bunch of humans there—with food—putting out the fire or trying to.) Sure enough, when I arrived back at the fire scene the bear was foraging around in the smoke jumpers' backpacks for lunch, and they were all up in trees, so they didn't become lunch themselves.

I maneuvered the helicopter around, herding the beast away so the men could get back to work. The bear didn't like being disturbed. At one point he turned around and stood up to take me on. He was a lot bigger than I'd expected at six or seven feet tall. I hovered to within fifteen feet of him before he thought perhaps, discretion being the better part of valor, he'd turn tail and run. I chased the bear up the hill and the crew went back to fighting the now growing fire. So, if an employer ever asks about my bear-chasing skill, I have the certification in my logbook.

At the end of the summer fire season, late August in that

part of the world, the company told me to bring the aircraft back to Anchorage.

To get there from Lake Minchumina, where I was based, required me to fly through Rainy Pass, near the middle of the Alaska Range, the chain of mountains that's the spine of Alaska stretching 600 miles from the Canadian border to the Aleutian Islands. The highest peak in the Alaska Range is Mt. Denali. (It was once called Mt. McKinley, but has been changed to *Denali*, the Koyukon peoples' word meaning "The Great One.")

As I said, it had been a wet summer in Alaska, which explained why the flight hours were minimal, with not much firefighting to do. But as I headed east across Rainy Pass, the sky was crystal clear, and as blue as I'd ever seen before or since. There must be something in the atmosphere in Alaska that turns the sky that color, but I couldn't tell you what it is.

At 5,000 feet above sea level to clear the terrain, alone in the aircraft, I entered Rainy Pass, a zig-zag route through the mountains fifty miles northwest of Anchorage. As I reached the center of the pass, out both sides of the cockpit lay the Alaska Range stretched from one end to the other, all 600 miles of it.

Awe inspiring is too tame and cliché. I soaked in the view, realizing that it was those experiences that had prompted me to fly in the first place. I regret that I carried no camera that day. But that was okay. No photo could have done it justice, and many years later I still have the image in my head.

Halfway through Rainy Pass I looked below at the remote and hostile terrain, at the rugged mountains on either side, and I understood the stories I'd heard about pilots flying in Alaska going down and never being seen again. Before my transit of Rainy Pass I'd considered those stories apocryphal, just the drunken ravings of braggart pilots in the Land of the Midnight Sun. But seeing how remote and inaccessible the terrain was, convinced me otherwise. If I'd gone down that day, they might be looking for me still.

Unless you've seen the Aurora Borealis you can't appreciate just how beautiful the natural world can be. If you've seen it from the front office of an aircraft, you know that feeling and more. There's simply no grander view.

In the summer of '74, I was flying a Huey for the Ohio National Guard, en route from a fuel stop in Lansing Michigan to the Annual Training site at Grayling. I'd left Lansing at dusk heading north and had leveled off at 2,000 feet on a balmy summer evening.

When the city lights of Lansing disappeared behind me, the light show started: Swaths of pastels, a curtain of illumination sweeping the horizon west to east and back again. Watching that light show gave me goose flesh. I couldn't stop looking at it, feasting on the exquisite vision stretching in front

CHAPTER 9: HIGH POINTS

of me. The vast, miles-high facade of pinks, and greens, and turquoise, and yellows washed the sky, sweeping and folding like a mammoth curtain of light. It was mesmerizing.

Too soon, Grayling crept into view, and I had to land. But the lights that night over central Michigan were a real high point in my career.

Scattered among the high points were some things that are hard to articulate their effect on me. One was the first time I took my father flying. Years before, dad had dismissed his own dream of flight to put groceries on the table for me, and my nine siblings. So, putting him in the cockpit with me that day was a real treat. As I took off on a Thanksgiving Day electronic newsgathering (ENG) job around St. Louis, dad's smile stretched across his rugged face. As he sat in the cockpit with me, his pilot son, arms folded, he was a truly happy man. When a tear trickled down his cheek—I don't know if he was mourning his own lost flying dream or reveling in his son's acquiring his own—my tears welled up. That flight was a wonderful bond we shared, and something I'll always cherish.

Other events were almost as gratifying: I received a letter from a fellow named Walter L who'd been badly injured as a seven-year-old in a farm accident. The night I flew Walter from a tiny hospital in northern Iowa he was not expected to live. He'd experienced massive trauma, had lost a lot of blood, and had sustained multiple orthopedic injuries. But Walter survived, and years later he wrote to thank me. Reading his letter was simply delightful, especially since, as he wrote, he'd married and had a seven-year-old son of his own. There's something deeply gratifying in using our skills to make someone's life better. Walter's letter is in my "most-memorable" file.

Here's another high point, a very short but, to me, very memorable episode in my flying career, and I wasn't in the cockpit at the time. First, let me go back a few years to when I was fourteen, wholly enthralled by the space race and specifically enchanted with NASA's Mercury program.

I was standing on the beach in Florida. It was February 20, 1962 at about 10:30 in the morning. I'd traveled south with mom and dad to escape the Ohio winter, and to (hopefully) be somewhere near Cape Canaveral if and when John Glenn's flight in Friendship 7 took off.

We drove south along the main highway that morning, listening on the car radio in our tiny Ford Falcon. At about 10:30 a.m., the radio announcer switched over to mission control, and dad pulled off the highway. Every other car had done the same. There was no traffic moving, as everyone had left their vehicles

CHAPTER 9: HIGH POINTS

and gone to the beach. We all stared north toward the Cape only a few miles away.

From the car radio I heard the final countdown, "ten-nine-eight-seven-six…" I shielded my eyes from the morning sun and looked toward the Cape. I was about to witness aviation history, "Five-four-three-two-one…"

Five or six more seconds elapsed. Then I saw it. The Atlas booster, with Glenn's black capsule atop, the orange-red escape tower on top of that, lifted on its white plume, arced over sideways, streaked across the morning sky higher and higher until it became a pin-point of reddish fire soaring downrange. Glenn was in space. We stared skyward until Friendship 7 disappeared into the mist. Then we all returned to our cars and went on our way. I never quite looked away from the sky again.

MY MOST CHERISHED LOGBOOK ENDORSEMENT

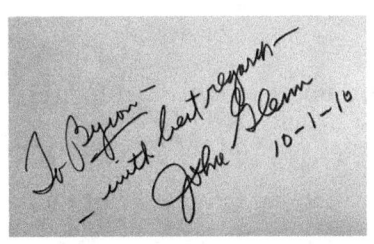

Flash forward forty-eight years. I'm at a fundraising event, and the key speaker is Col. John H. Glenn Jr. I managed to get his attention and asked if he'd sign my logbook. He took the book, scribbled the autograph and message above, and we swapped aviation stories for a few minutes. I mentioned to him that I'd seen his launch that long-ago morning and that his actions had spurred me toward a life in the sky. I suspected he'd heard people say the same thing, but he accepted the statement, and soon moved on to other people.

John Glenn's inscription in my logbook is one of my prized possessions, and what I told Col. Glenn that day is true. It was heroes like him who affirmed my dream to fly. Meeting him was truly one of the high points of my career.

**Flying is hours and hours of boredom
interrupted by moments of...hysteria!**

One of the yuk-yuk funniest things that happened to me occurred in Vietnam. I was in the left seat of the Huey, on a combat assault into a small LZ, the third aircraft in a formation of six. The LZ was hot. Both aircraft in front of me had reported taking fire going in and coming out. I alerted my crew, and started down for the LZ.

I told my crew to start their suppressive fire, but to keep it off the LZ because American troops were on the ground. A few seconds later both 30. caliber machine guns erupted, hot rounds barking out and making a god-awful racket that blasted in my headset.

Suddenly, the gunner's M-60 stopped. Then the oddest thing: I heard a whistle. Like the referee's at a Friday night football game, it bleated again and again. What the..?

CHAPTER 9: HIGH POINTS

I landed in the LZ, the grunts hopped off the aircraft, and I looked back at the door gunner, a guy named John Mabry. He was tweeting away on the whistle, while jerking his gun's loading rod back and forth. "Mabry!" I said. "What the hell are you doing? And what's with the whistle?"

"My gun jammed, sir!" he said. "I was callin' time out!"[13]

One of the most satisfying events was the day I left Vietnam to return "to the world" as we said. When the big 707 taxied from the terminal at Cam Ranh Bay on March 17, 1971, I sat with my fellow returning Vietnam vets waiting for takeoff. It had been a long year, with lots of bad missions, lost friends, frightening incidents, and the depressing reality that the Vietnam War was likely a lost cause for us. So, when the freedom bird left the ground that day the ear-splitting roar of celebration echoed through the cabin, a cascade of joyous energy rivaling the roaring jet engines outside. That was truly one of the high points of my flying career, and I wasn't even flying.

Landing in a simulator is like kissing your sister.
—An old pilot

One of the more gratifying events of my career happened in a simulator. The sim I was flying at the time was for a Boeing

CH-47 Chinook. That afternoon I showed myself and the fellow who was my instructor that, after thirty years of flying, I'd learned a thing or two, while proving the old aviation admonition to never stop flying the aircraft. You can be a pilot, or you can be a passenger. You can't be both.

I was in the left seat of the Chinook simulator, and the instructor pilot (IP) was seated at the console directly behind me. The sim for the Chinook is a highly sophisticated, $30-million device with full visuals, six degrees of motion, and the ability to simulate every aircraft emergency, malfunction, and flight condition, including a few that were so far-fetched we'd laugh about them. Well, the IP almost got the last laugh from me that day. Almost.

The flight proceeded with the standard startup and operation procedures for the Chinook, followed by simulations of flight in turbulence, icing, extreme low visibility, instrument approaches to low minimums, and a few other parameters. Then we went on to EPs, emergency procedures.

The IP threw in malfunctions. He tossed a fuselage fire at me, then an electrical failure, an oil leak, a hydraulic malfunction, a runaway engine governor, and a failure of the AFCS, the Hook's automatic stabilizing system. I handled all the malfunctions well, using the checklist, addressing each failure and emergency.

CHAPTER 9: HIGH POINTS

With the session nearly over, we headed back to the fake airfield, and the IP decided to see how good I was at handling multiple failures. First, he took away the hydraulics, so I had to start the auxiliary power unit (APU) to get them back. Then he failed the number two engine. The automatic flight control system (AFCS) failed, again. Then the fuselage caught fire... again. On top of that, we started taking enemy fire from a rocket-propelled grenade (RPG), which hit us in the side of our simulated aircraft. The Chinook was still flying, so I kept going, with the simulated airfield's fake runway a mile ahead.

The most important sequence in aviation got me there: Aviate, Navigate, Communicate. Never stop flying the aircraft. Only after regaining control should, you navigate. Once you're oriented, only then communicate. All three are important; but the order is most important.

The IP tried everything he could think of to force me down. Another fire, then a generator failure, a torque system malfunction. The tachometer failed. Half the gauges had some kind of anomaly. The caution panel looked like a pinball board. Nothing did the trick. I did what I'd been trained to do; I flew the sucker till it wouldn't fly anymore.

With one remaining engine still burning and turning, I limped toward the airfield as altitude fell off, and airspeed dropped below single engine minimum. I kept flying anyway.

The IP hounded me: *"Never make it, Edgington. No way you'll get this thing on the ground. No way!"*

But I did. I managed to plant the wheels of the Chinook on the fake runway's first painted stripes and rolled out. Shaking his head in disbelief, the IP failed the Chinook's remaining engine, and we coasted to a stop with no hydraulics, no electric power, and nothing showing on the black dark panel. But I landed.

I'd tried to get into Chinook training right after flight school. I'm glad I didn't. My tour in Vietnam flying a Huey was a much better fit for me. Near retirement though, I got the chance to fly the 'Hook, and discovered that it isn't just two Hueys snapped together. The Chinook is a highly complex, maintenance-intensive, heavily systematized and crew-served aircraft that's a real pleasure to fly. But it also has 100 different ways it can kill you. Learning to fly it when I did made me a forty-eight-year-old rookie, but I did well with it despite that, (because of that?) I'd picked up a few tricks along the way. It was beyond gratifying to put that aircraft on the runway that day, even if it was only simulated.

Last, flying the Na Pali Coast of Kauai. As I flew this coastline, the rugged, verdant terrain stretching a thousand feet down the lush, tropical cliffs, ending at the sea-battered beach

CHAPTER 9: HIGH POINTS

below. I couldn't stop looking at it, feasting on the exquisite vision stretching in front of me. It was almost shameful that I was being paid to do so. If you've not seen the Na Pali Coast of Kauai, do it right away, regardless of the cost, or convenience, or interruption in your daily life. It is a must see.

There's grandeur, joy, and affirmation, and beauty in every flight. It's up to us to find it.

Lessons:
- If you're not aware of the beauty of flying, go back to work.
- No matter how many hours in the logbook, you'll always be a rookie, and that's a good thing.
- Big aircraft are fun; smaller aircraft can be more fun.
- Fly it to the ground. Never give up!
- The most important sequence: Aviate, Navigate, Communicate.

—*An old pilot*

Chapter 10

LOW POINTS

Bell 206 Jet Ranger
Pole-mark pole...Pole-mark pole...

A s a pilot, I never worked a day in my life. No matter what job I found myself in, or what mission I was assigned, I was grateful for my good fortune, and for the opportunity to do what I loved. I couldn't believe they paid me to fly.

However, sometimes I couldn't believe how *little* they paid me to fly. Those days were few and far between, but I had more than one of them. The following are some of those low-paying, low satisfaction assignments. These jobs may have been humiliating, quixotic adventures, but they all contained a lesson.

I was flying for Helicopters Incorporated.[14] Heli-Inc. is a fine company near St. Louis that threw many amazing and challenging jobs my way. In one particular posting, flying a Bell 206 Jet Ranger, I counted power poles all day. The helicopter was outfitted with camera and GPS locator equipment attached under its belly. The client was American Electric Power (AEP) a major electricity provider in the Northeast. The assignment was to stamp each one of AEP's thousands of power poles with GPS data, and then take its picture. Before I flew the AEP job, I'd thought power poles looked pretty much alike, but apparently not.

Here's how my day went: I was in the Jet Ranger's right seat. The AEP guy sat in the left seat. In the back a fellow had a TV screen in front of him, keeping his finger on the GPS marking button/camera. I cruised along the power lines at

CHAPTER 10: LOW POINTS

twice the height of the poles. I could fly no faster than thirty knots, or the GPS equipment dropped the signal. As each pole slid beneath the nose of the aircraft the left-seater said, "Pole." When the back-seater saw the pole appear on his TV screen, he responded, "Mark pole." Then he'd mash his button, take the pole's photo, and assign it a GPS position. *"Pole-mark pole...pole, mark pole..."*

All day long, for three months, I sat in the cockpit, practically hovering along, listening to "Pole—Mark pole. Pole—Mark pole. Pole..." You get the idea. It sounded like kids in a swimming pool with their irritating Marco! Polo! I started hearing "Pole—Mark pole" in my sleep.

But it was a job, and I was happy to help my employer out. I was also extremely happy when the pole counting gig ended. After a few weeks hearing "Pole—Mark pole" all day, I decided the job could better be done by a low-time pilot, a rookie eager for a chance to pile hours in their logbook. I was flying on average seven hours every day. That was a lot of turbine time that a rookie pilot would love to have.

Then one morning I encountered a situation that tested my years of experience, a perilous event that took all my expertise to handle. It was as close to a wire strike as I ever came.

I was cruising through a valley at 8 a.m., heading east into the morning sun along a power line, when I noticed a lone power pole atop a ridge. Something in my experience data bank grabbed my attention, and I stopped the aircraft at a hover. Then I glanced across the valley to the opposite ridge. Sure enough, there was another pole.

The AEP guys asked what was up. "There's got to be a wire here somewhere," I said, squinting into the morning glare. And there it was. Thirty feet in front of me, a double power line stretched across my flight path. Had I continued forward, I'd have flown right into it.

So, I was grateful in an odd sort of way that I'd been in that cockpit, and the rookie I'd wanted to gift all those hours to wasn't. Hitting a wire in a helicopter will ruin your day.[15]

One of my instructors in flight school told me I'd be okay in Vietnam until I'd flown roughly 500 hours. "Edgington," he'd said, "When you first get there, still pissin' stateside water, the veteran guys won't let you fly anyway, so you can't hurt yourself. But when you get to be an AC, with about 500 hours of flight time you'll think you're the flyin' god's gift to aviation, and that's when you'll get yourself in trouble."

Well, he was right. I was in the left seat of the Huey heading into an LZ on a muggy, miserably hot July afternoon. Behind me on the cargo floor of the helicopter sat 1,000 pounds of well-fed, heavily outfitted U.S. troops, five men weighing

CHAPTER 10: LOW POINTS

altogether half a metric ton waiting for me to land so they could go to work against the enemy.

In addition, I had a full bag of jet fuel, adding about 1,000 more pounds to the Huey's weight. The guys who'd landed ahead of me in the LZ reported that the wind was shifting around, first from the west, then 180 degrees the other way, due east. I was the number four ship that day, and watching the other pilots land, it seemed they'd each picked a different access.

It was my turn. Considering the weight of the helicopter, the muggy conditions, (helicopters don't like hot and heavy), I made a slow, deliberate approach to the LZ. As I descended, I could feel the wind shifting around, kicking my tail this way and that. It was about to kick my tail really hard.

On short final, the Huey shuddered, which made me glance at the gauges. A chill ran up my arms when I looked at the airspeed needle, and saw it pasted on zero! No wonder the aircraft shook like that, I thought. I'm essentially hovering into the LZ.

Fifty feet off the ground, I was still descending 400 feet per minute, and the vertical speed indicator (VSI) needle kept dropping. The torque gauge showed my power at forty-seven pounds, with fifty pounds being the limit. Then, twenty feet off the ground, it felt like a giant hand shoved me down onto the LZ. I landed short, and hard, and sooner than I'd wanted to. That landing would have given me a score of ten—on the Richter scale!

The Huey slammed onto the LZ, dirt and dust flew everywhere, and the aircraft rocked back and forth at the sloped edge of the landing zone.

Then the fun started. The heavy troops leapt off. When they did, the much lighter Huey tried to take off again, only backward off the edge of the LZ! I shoved the cyclic forward to stop it from flipping over, but that input set up a vibration in the rotor head caused by a condition called mast bumping. Finally, I managed to get control, took off with my tail between my legs, thankful that I hadn't destroyed a perfectly good Huey. On takeoff, my old instructor's warning echoed in my head, "At 500 hours, you'll think you're god's gift to aviation, that's when you'll hurt yourself!" I realized he was right. My 759, the form that tracks Army flight hours, showed I'd logged just over 500 hours of time in the cockpit.

Heading back to base I didn't feel like god's gift to aviation. I felt like the dumb, inexperienced rookie pilot that I was. That incident may have been the best thing that happened in my career. It showed that I wasn't invulnerable, and that older, wiser pilots often know what they're talking about.

The way you're first taught and learn a procedure is the way you'll react in an emergency. It's important to learn it right the first time.

—An old pilot

CHAPTER 10: LOW POINTS

This is a good place to add a reflection on safety and the best way to pursue a long, safe, trouble-free career in aviation. One way to do that, as counterintuitive as it sounds, is to stay a bit afraid.

We don't associate pilots with fear. When we see aviators strolling through airports, or strutting across flight lines, we see people who carry themselves with confidence and certainty. They approach the aircraft with an air of assurance that they know the machine's limits and their own. They know how to handle deviations in the norm. They appear to know what they're doing.

When I flew for a living, I walked and strutted like that, too. I made an effort to show a degree of confidence that I sometimes didn't have. It's not fair to your passengers to appear afraid, or to talk of uncertainty, or to display hesitation. No airline passenger wants to hear their pilot say, "Well, folks, we have a little problem up here in the front office, and we're not sure what to do about it." That kind of announcement can start a mutiny.

Even so, I can attest that one of the reasons I had a safe, incident/accident-free career was that I always maintained a degree of fear. It was never debilitating or paralyzing. The feeling never had me follow a course that made things worse or caused me to give up on a particular operation. It was a healthy fear, a simple concession to the complexity and power of the aircraft, and the forces acting on it. It was a deep and abiding respect for what could happen and how quickly and how little control I might have if certain things went south.

Maybe it was more *respect* than fear. Becoming a pilot is a wondrous thing, full of amazing rewards and benefits. It's a prestigious position that few people have the opportunity to achieve, and a degree of respect will help any pilot honor that.

As I dusted myself off that day following my LZ adventure, hearing my old instructor's warning, I felt the gratitude that came with my escape from a near accident. I felt a degree of embarrassment and the first premonitions of the fear I mentioned. I saw how quickly I could be overwhelmed by forces I couldn't foresee or control. It was an excellent lesson, and I learned it well.

As for other low points in my career, one was 9/11, and the impact that awful day had on aviation. That Tuesday morning in September 2001, I'd reported for duty at the hospital. Just as it was in New York City, the autumn Iowa sky was clear and cool, with the first hint of fall. A beautiful day to fly.

Of course, the events of the next several hours changed all that. They changed the world, in ways we still haven't quite discerned twenty years later. I watched the towers fall, saw the evil plume of dust envelop lower Manhattan, and gaped wide-eyed at the destruction caused by two aircraft. Clearly the pilots involved had very different priorities from mine. I was posted to an air medical position, flying a rescue helicopter to *save* lives; those pilots had taken off that day to *destroy* as many lives as they could.

As I watched the horror of 9/11 unfold, the phone rang. It was the company chief pilot, "Do not fly that helicopter," he said. "If you get a call, do not take it. Stay on the ground until further notice."

I told the dispatcher we were grounded. Three days later, the FAA allowed selective flying in the national airspace system. One entity allowed back in the air was medical helicopters, so I was permitted to accept emergency calls. But in order to accept a flight I had certain restrictions: I was given a specific squawk code and I had to report every takeoff and landing to ATC.

The first flight after 9/11 was unlike any I'd ever taken. Instead of the constant chatter across the radios, continuous interactions with ATC, and the ever-present contrails high above, the sky was empty, and the radios were silent. In that silent sky, I flew my team and patient back to the hospital and landed uneventfully. But that day stands out as a low point.

During that terrible time, I reflected a bit on aviation's place in our culture, and how that position of status had been used and abused by the bastards who flew the planes into those buildings. The contrast was shocking. I thought about all the flying I'd done and the way I'd conducted myself in the cockpit. I thought of how those nineteen men had used the assets I'd made the center of my livelihood to wreak such destruction. Mostly, I thought about that silent sky and how we take flying for granted. Maybe we shouldn't.

The lowest low point of my aviation career came on December 5, 2005, the day I was forced from the cockpit.

I was flying tours on Kauai and was on top of my game in every way. I lived in the most beautiful place on earth. I was paid a lot of money to cruise around the island every day while showing its breathtaking splendor to people. I'd reached a level of expertise in the cockpit that put me at the top of my profession.

An old aviation adage states that if you don't think you're the best in the game, you're in the wrong game. Well, on that fateful day, I was the best in the game and the best pilot in the sky. What happened on my fourth tour changed everything. I went from the top of the world to the depths of despair.

Near the end of the tour, I crossed a ridgeline on the north shore of Kauai and cruised in front of a waterfall named NaMaLokama. A centerpiece of the tour, Namo features the highest continuous waterfall on earth, plummeting 2,300 feet. Namo was spectacular that December afternoon, so I cruised

CHAPTER 10: LOW POINTS

in front of it slowly, allowing my six passengers to stare and shoot pictures. Out of the blue, I had a sudden and completely unexpected episode of near syncope. I saw stars. My vision narrowed. I felt lightheaded. I almost passed out. Fighting to stay awake, I breathed deeply, clenched my stomach, and shook my head to stay conscious. Finally, sweaty with fear, I felt the episode ease and go away.

The event scared me to my boots. If I'd passed out that day I would have gone down and taken six people with me. It would have been one of those inexplicable accidents, a crushed pile of helicopter rubble that no one could explain. I finished the tour, landed, and stepped out of the cockpit. For the last time.

It's been fifteen years since that low point, and I can now say a couple of things about it. First, I'm grateful for the outcome, because it could have been a lot worse. Second, though I miss flying every day, I have my health, and the love of a woman who stands by me no matter what. That's not nothing. Third, I have respect for myself, and the decision to not take off again that day. After the episode of dizziness went away, I felt fine. Like nothing had happened. I could have climbed into the cockpit, taken off, and continued flying as usual.

I didn't. Why not? Because all the safe, incident, and accident free flying I'd done up to that point lobbied against it. At that point I'd flown helicopters for almost fifty years. I'd logged 12,500 hours of safe flying. I'd never scratched the paint on an aircraft; I'd never hurt anyone. I wasn't about to jeopardize my record. It was the hardest thing I ever had to do, but I hung up my headset, and have not flown since.

Lessons:
- There will be low points.
- Never take your career for granted.
- A safe, accident free/incident free career is priceless—and achievable.
- When it's time to give it up, you will know.
- At a certain number of hours logged, you'll think you're wholly competent. This is the time to be very cautious because you're not.
- The high points will teach you many things. The low points will teach you more.

—*An old pilot*

Chapter 11
CARE & FEEDING OF YOUR MECHANIC

AS 319 Alouette
An ungainly looking machine, but really strong

Mechanic: Someone smart enough to take it apart, clever enough to hide the extra parts when he's done.

The care and feeding of an aircraft mechanic may sound straightforward. You interact with them over broken aircraft pieces and parts, or sticky and glitchy systems. You write the malfunction up on the proper form. You scribble your name on it. You leave them alone with their mystical magical tool kit and head for the showers. Right? What could be simpler? This chapter may be the key to a rookie pilot's success, or lack of it, in the attention paid to the mechanic.

I'm not blowing smoke when I say that mechanics are the most underrated people in aviation. They work at least as long as pilots do, for less money, often late into the night, and often with less protection from feckless or type A bosses who want the damn aircraft fixed and out the door like yesterday.

I became aware of the tough job the wrench benders had only after I started flying commercially. Interacting with them on job sites, and in hangar settings, I realized that I'd not paid much attention to mechanics in my military life. The first thing I had to assimilate to was the fact that often there was only one mechanic assigned to the aircraft. There was no "maintenance staff" like in the military. The maintenance staff consisted of one dude, although these days I'm sure there are dudettes in the mechanic ranks.

Especially in Air Medical flying, I had to be sensitive to my mechanic's FAA crew rest status and not pester the poor

CHAPTER 11: CARE & FEEDING OF YOUR MECHANIC

fellow to schlep into the hospital at oh-dark-thirty to fix a burned-out light bulb. As marginally legal as it was, I learned to do certain minor maintenance items myself and to have the guy with proper tools and the A&P license sign off my work in the morning. The FAA may have frowned on that, but it wasn't like I'd changed an engine by myself. I was only being considerate of the guy who kept things turning and burning. It was the least I could do. Still, it took a bit of time to adjust to it.

Being aware of my mechanic made me more cautious with the equipment as well. Overstressing and abusing an aircraft is not only dangerous but also disrespectful to the mechanic. The stress and exertion on parts and systems may not show up right away but it will manifest eventually. Whoever is in charge of fixing it when it breaks may not appreciate the added work, especially if life limits on certain parts aren't met, and replacement has to happen earlier than the planned mean time between failures (MTBF). The owner or operator won't appreciate it much either, and those folks do sign the paychecks.

There were, admittedly, times I pushed boundaries with a helicopter, either to get the job done, or to amend a bad situation. An experience in Vietnam comes to mind. The landing zone I'd been given was much too small for the Huey, so I used the rotor blades to trim a few (very thin) tree limbs surrounding it. Gil, my mechanic/crew chief, didn't like my pruning activity very much, but he understood it, and it didn't damage the blades.

Once, in an AStar, I had a sticky fuel gauge needle, which I fixed in a rather unconventional fashion. When I started the engine, after topping off the tank, the fuel needle stuck for about the third time in that aircraft. So, I lifted to a relatively low hover, and then dropped the collective quickly, banging the skids on the concrete. After the third bang, the fuel needle unstuck itself, and crept up the gauge. The mechanic was with me at the time. He approved the procedure, though I doubt you'll find it posted in an operator's manual.

Another war story. This tale doesn't seem to connect with the care and feeding of a mechanic, but as you read along, you'll agree that it does. Considering that, No. 1, Gil my crew chief/mechanic was on board with me that day, and No. 2, he had to deal with the damage later it's obvious that the "war story" fits this chapter. I'm still embarrassed about what happened, even though the event took place half a century ago, in a land far away where rice is served with every meal. Here's what happened:

My crew and I had finished our assigned missions and were heading home, when a group of troopers radioed, asking me to do a sling load detail for them. The small contingent of troops was aboard a small raft positioned in a twenty-acre bay. The little gun platform on the water was perhaps the size of a tennis court. On it sat a quad-50, a four-barrel, 50. caliber machine gun that those

CHAPTER 11: CARE & FEEDING OF YOUR MECHANIC

troops used to guard the railroad tracks running alongside the bay. The quad-50 was inoperative. They'd called me to lift it off the deck, and to fly it into Phu Bai for maintenance.

The plan was to hover above the big gun, then latch it onto the Huey's cargo hook. I'd pick it up, and away we'd go. Well... things did not go to plan, as the Brits often say.

I hovered above the gun using a corner of the raft as a reference point, while the troops beneath the helicopter put the lifting cable onto the cargo hook. With that done, they gave the thumbs up, and Gil told me to go ahead and lift it off the deck.

It only sounds easy. As I rose to a higher hover, I lost my reference point on the boat's deck, and was then hovering over water, which is a damnably difficult thing to do because, with the rotor downwash whipping up the water, it's almost impossible to find a hovering reference point.

I noticed that the torque gauge was rising much faster than I'd anticipated, which meant the gun was a lot heavier than I thought. As I wrestled with the quad-50, trying to lift it off the deck, I watched the torque climb past forty, to forty-five, to almost fifty pounds, the red line! I began to wonder, "how frickin' heavy is that damn gun?"

Gil announced our progress, and it was not looking good. I'd drifted forward over the water, and the lifting cable was angled in such a way that, had I managed to bring that heavy gun up, it may have slipped off the deck into the water, taking us down with it.

Finally, I had the good sense to release the cable, and to reassess the situation. I punched it off and landed back on the raft. Then I told those troops I was sorry, but we couldn't help them with their broken quad-50. They'd have to call a Chinook outfit instead.

On the flight home, I thought about what might have happened. If that gun had slid into the water, it would have taken me down with it much faster than I could have punched it off. If I'd gone into the water, the Huey would have been lost, and my crew could have drowned. I kicked myself for not thinking the scenario through, for assuming too much, and for taking that kind of chance when it wasn't even a hostile environment. The only hostility that day was my own wrestling with my dangerous "can-do" attitude. It nearly got me killed. The fact that I'd called time out and stopped what I was doing was cold comfort.

Here's where my mechanic gets involved. No. 1, he was in the aircraft with me, so if I'd had an accident that day Gil was along for the ride. No. 2, by trying to lift that heavy gun I overstressed the Huey's cargo hook, and Gil had to work extra hours to repair it. In other words, I wasn't thinking about his role in the near disaster, possibly the closest I've come to destroying a helicopter and killing my crew.

CHAPTER 11: CARE & FEEDING OF YOUR MECHANIC

Your mechanics will likely not be aboard the aircraft as you pursue your daily assignments. Perhaps the best way to care for them is to fly as if they *were* aboard, watching how you treat *their* machine. Some mechanics will tell you that the aircraft belongs to them; they just allow you to fly it, provided you take care of it. That sounds about right.

Here's a list of ways to write up squawks. It's a template that can help your mechanic diagnose the problem.

1. When and where did you first notice the glitch?
2. Were there indications prior to failure?
3. Did it surge, or has it been intermittent?
4. If it's a cycling system, how often is it supposed to cycle?
5. For radios: range of transmission/reception before?
6. Did you notice unusual noises in the headset/helmet?
7. Did you feel any vibrations, looseness, or stiffness in controls?
8. Notice any smoke or fumes?
9. What did the generator/alternator do?
10. Leakage, lower/higher pressure, variations in other gauges?

Address every malfunction and failure in the aircraft this way, adding as much information as you think is necessary, plus some you're not sure of, and your mechanic will thank you for it. Nothing upsets them more than vague, inefficient, and useless write-ups. Write as much as you can, and be specific; it makes the mechanic's job a lot easier.

This tip isn't exactly maintenance-related, but it will help keep you safe. Your instructor has no doubt shown you how to do a thorough preflight check of the aircraft. Here are a few things to consider, regardless of what aircraft you're about to fly:

An important part of your preflight routine is the simple walkaround inspection. It's easy to go to the aircraft, look over the logbook, drain the fuel sumps, remove the tie-downs and wheel chocks, take off the *Remove Before Flight* tags and hop into the cockpit. Before you board, do another walkaround. Look at the aircraft closely. Look at latches, air intakes, reservoir caps, movable surfaces, and the general condition of the aircraft. Check the ground underneath it for suspicious fluid leaks. For a night flight, check the condition and operation of lights.

It's also a good habit to tune into the emergency radio frequency, and test the Emergency Locator Transmitter, (ELT), on either 121.5 VHF, 243.0 UHF, or for newer ELTs 406 MhZ. Check all the seat locks to make sure they're secure for takeoff, that the windows are clean, and the door latches work properly. Then walk around again. You'll be glad you did.

CHAPTER 11: CARE & FEEDING OF YOUR MECHANIC

Lessons:
- Mechanics are your friends. Treat them well.
- The best way to treat a mechanic well is to treat the aircraft well.
- Describing the glitch precisely helps a lot. Write-ups for noises, and shimmies, and vibrations, and hiccups aren't helpful.
- Don't break rules, but don't bring your mechanic in at 3 AM for a busted lightbulb, either. Change it yourself or wait till morning.
- Help them with the work. You'll learn a lot.
- Take them flying. They rarely ask and few pilots offer.
- Don't boggle up the paperwork. (See the template above).
- Never blame a mechanic for your screwup. Never.
- Pay attention to pending inspections, and don't overfly them.
- The mechanic has a license to lose, too.

—An old pilot

Chapter 12

CARE & FEEDING OF PASSENGERS

AS 350 B2 AStar/H-125

The strength of turbulence is directly proportional to the temperature of your coffee.

—*Anonymous*

Regardless of whether you're flying military or commercial, you need to be aware of your passengers. They're along for the ride, and wholly dependent on your skills and judgment. In any kind of flight condition, any weather, day or night, it's nice to have a set of controls and some input on what happens to the aircraft. You do; passengers don't. Always be aware of that.

The Huey I flew in Vietnam had an armored seat. One side of the seat held an armored plate that slid forward and back, to allow the pilot to enter the cockpit. If I forgot to slide that armor into place, and then needed its protection going into a hot LZ, I'd just grab it, and slide it forward.

But when I did that, it sent a signal to the troops behind me that there was danger ahead and they reacted accordingly. I'd slide the armor forward, and then I'd hear groans and curses from the infantry guys. I realized that they didn't need any further aggravation, so I started using the armor all the time.

When I flew tourists on Kauai, one of the more common questions came from nervous passengers who'd ask about the wet weather. Kauai is a rainy place, and rain could and did interfere with visibility, so the question was not without merit.

I had to be diplomatic in my answer. There were passengers who were genuinely afraid to fly, wishing to go only in ideal weather, so I had to try different tactics with them. For some, it was enough to mention my Vietnam experience. I'd tell them that conditions were much worse over there than they were on Kauai and leave it at that. For some passengers, no amount of handholding worked; I had to take them flying to show that their fears were overstated.

Especially if you fly helicopters, machines that are much more maneuverable, it's difficult to ignore the temptation to wring the machine out and show off its various parameters. Near as I can figure, I flew upwards of half a million people in my career, and the percentage of those passengers who enjoyed that wild kind of flying was vanishingly small.

No one gets into aviation to have a stable, steady, monotonous life. Admit it, you want to fly because it's fun and exhilarating. Aspiring pilots like you are people who enjoy their freedom, and their ability to make their own way, unencumbered.

However, this feeling presents one of the conundrums of aviation: While flying is an amazing, often viscerally thrilling activity, your job as the pilot is to deliver "an uneventful flight," that is, a safe, almost boring passage from one place to another for the people riding behind you. Especially when you're new to the flying business, the temptation to wheel the aircraft through the sky, banking and careering just for the thrill of it, is likely the last thing your passengers want. It can be difficult for you to suppress the desire to fly the aircraft as you'd like to, in deference to people who don't share your enthusiasm for that kind of adventure. Avoid it anyway. In other words, fly for them, not for yourself. Here's an example of why you should.

Most of my tour passengers on Kauai had never been in a helicopter. They'd heard horror stories about how dangerous the aircraft are, and how many accidents they have, and yadda, yadda. On Kauai, there have been a spate of tour helicopter accidents through the years, so it was tough to assuage people's fears with innocuous dismissals. During my pre-flight briefing, I'd read their body language and watch their response to what I told them to assess their fear level.

At Air Kauai I typically flew with six passengers, mostly couples. They came from all over, mostly from the mainland US, and they were commonly newlyweds. I greeted a group of tourists one afternoon on the flight line. A woman named Wendy was in the group. Wendy was by herself, which was unusual. She quickly became one of my favorite passengers. Wendy was excited, quirky, funny, and fearless. She wore a headscarf, and she had several flower leis wrapped around her neck. Just seeing her toothy grin, I knew Wendy was eager to go flying and that the upcoming tour was going to be special. During the briefing, another woman asked me about the weather: "What about this rain?" she said. Wendy answered for me: "No rain, no rainbows!" Then she wagged her finger at me. "If I don't see a rainbow today, I want my money back!"

CHAPTER 12: CARE & FEEDING OF PASSENGERS

I told Wendy there were no guarantees, but I'd do what I could to find her a rainbow. I finished the briefing, then loaded folks aboard the helicopter, putting Wendy next to me in the cockpit. Shortly, we were flying around the island.

Wendy more or less took over the tour. She'd point at various things along the way and say, "Take me there," and "over there," and "I want to see that." I simply did as I was told. The other five passengers didn't seem to mind. It was a fun tour. Along the Na Pali coast, on Kauai's northwest side, I noticed a rainbow forming, so I increased airspeed in an effort to get into position for it.

Sure enough, the gorgeous bow formed perfectly, arcing its stunning colors across the lush background of the Na Pali coast, crashing waves and pristine beach below. It was a postcard-perfect display of Hawaii's natural beauty.

As I cruised in front of the rainbow, I looked at Wendy. "No refund for you." Instead of laughing, Wendy tapped my knee and she said, "Okay, I'm done. I can go now." Her grin had disappeared and a tear traced her cheek. "But the tour's only half over," I assured her. "It's all right," she said. "I can go now."

I finished the tour, landed, and offloaded my passengers. As they walked toward the bus, Wendy turned back, then she wandered over and gave me a peck on the cheek. "Thank you," she whispered. Then she was gone.[16]

A month later there was a letter in my in-box at the office. It was from the woman who'd accompanied Wendy to Kauai. She wrote to thank me for taking Wendy on the tour. Wendy had a wonderful time, the woman wrote, and she'd managed to get done everything she'd wanted to. The woman went on to tell me that Wendy had died two weeks after she flew with me and saw her rainbow, *the last item on her bucket list,* according to the letter. At that moment I understood what Wendy meant when she said, "I can go now". It all made sense. And it made me pay more attention to what my passengers were *really* saying.

Wendy's statement was a profound affirmation that your passengers deserve to be heard. As a pilot, you will hold a sacred responsibility to the people in your care. Not just because they pay the freight, but because they trust you with their lives—and sometimes with their bucket list items as it turns out—and they can show you why you wanted to fly in the first place.

I witnessed pilots flying beyond aircraft limits, exceeding standard turn and bank angles, and stressing the aircraft. I said nothing. I could duck behind the FAR 91.3 Pilot in Command rule, and claim it wasn't my place to reprimand a fellow pilot. But the truth is, I was too timid to speak up and confront their behavior.

You may become too attuned to the tribe mentality as well

CHAPTER 12: CARE & FEEDING OF PASSENGERS

and hesitate to criticize one of your colleagues. It will be a tough call for you but possibly necessary.

I'd suggest that some kind of comment mechanism might be in order, a place for you to critique others' performance, anonymously if nothing else.

One last note on cowboy pilots. I'll call it "combat pilot syndrome." I saw a few individuals in air medical aviation infected with it, and a few more in the tour flying business. Those men—they were all men—never quite returned from the various wars they'd been in. The influence of flying in combat can affect veteran pilots. The syndrome is characterized by a disregard for aircraft limits or maneuvering guidelines and the urge to push an aircraft to the limit just to accomplish the mission. Especially in air medical flying, this impulse can be insidious, dangerous, and unpredictable.

Since I retired, I understand the situation a bit better. First, because helicopter cockpits are typically single pilot, there's little chance for oversight. Secondly, pressure between pilots, operators, and the FAA to keep aircraft aloft, and to keep the cash coming in is immense. Operating an aircraft is very expensive. The machines make money only when they're airborne, and that requires a pilot. So, grounding a pilot, for whatever reason, throws sand in the gears. There's a financial incentive to disregard poor pilot performance and marginal skills. So, the last thing an operator is likely to do is take the word of a rookie over a seasoned pilot. The lesson to you is to fly to the best of your ability, avoid the cowboy (cowgirl?) label, and never be afraid to speak up, or to walk away if you feel unsafe.

Another consideration when you're flying passengers is airsickness. It sounds like a minor issue, something you should overlook and let passengers tend to. But your obligation includes their physical comfort as well. You don't want to find out later that your customer had a lousy experience because of nausea, or any other physical discomfort, not to mention the possibility of having a major cleanup exercise after your flight.

When I was a new tour pilot on Kauai, veteran pilots told me that passenger airsickness was a real consideration. The farthest windward of the Hawaiian island chain, Kauai has the most violent turbulence of any place I'd ever flown. Many times, on windy days I'd take off for a tour, only to cancel it shortly after takeoff because my passengers would be bumped around so much it wasn't worth continuing.

An inexpensive cure for nausea is ginger candy. I always kept a bag of it on board the helicopter. I'd offer it to passengers prior to liftoff, telling them it was to take care of any tummy issue they may have, and it worked like a charm. Whether it kept them nausea-free because of the ginger, or because I'd changed their expectation, I don't know. But it worked.

CHAPTER 12: CARE & FEEDING OF PASSENGERS

Something else I did on my tours was to include passengers as much as possible, memorizing their names, checking their comfort level throughout the tour, and by being accessible to them.

Concern for passengers was especially important, ironically, when I was flying medical patients, most of whom were unconscious. One of the things I enjoyed most as an air medical pilot was the criticality of the mission. In the twenty years I flew at a hospital, I never flew one nosebleed victim or sprained ankle. My customers were critically ill people. So, it was especially important to take extra care of them and of the flight crews caring for them who put their lives in my hands. It was in air medical flying that I really observed the maxim that *the best flight is an uneventful flight.*

I ignored my own counsel about passenger considerations one time, and I regret it even today. It concerned a fellow named Howard. He was a patient on my helicopter one January night after crashing his Trans Am into a tree. Howard broke nearly every bone he owned, and he had internal injuries that the rural hospital couldn't address. So, they'd called the medical helicopter. My flight nurse and I landed to transport Howard at about midnight.

As badly injured as Howard was, he was still conscious. As

you might imagine he was in a lot of pain. But he was royally pissed off, because he'd been told that a helicopter was coming for him and he wanted no part of flying. He screamed, cursed, and he tried to kick off his restraints. While my flight nurse and I loaded him inside the helicopter, he spat at us, called us names, cursed us, and generally made a nuisance of himself.

The forty-minute flight to the big hospital was more of the same. Howard continued kicking and screaming and spitting. At one point he even threatened to jump out.

When I landed at the hospital, Howard immediately fell silent. Breathing deeply, with tears in his eyes, he simply stared at me. I thought, what the..? When the medical team wheeled him away, he asked them to stop, and called out. "Hey, pilot!" he yelled. I wandered next to his side. "What can I do for you?" He stared at me again. "Sorry for all the yellin' and shit," he said. "My daddy was killed in Vietnam on a helicopter, and I was really scared."

The late Robin Williams once said that everyone is fighting a battle we know nothing about, so always choose to be kind. Howard showed me how true that is. Your passengers may have their own fears and anxieties, so always treat them well. And always listen, especially to what they *don't* say.

CHAPTER 12: CARE & FEEDING OF PASSENGERS

Lessons:
- Listen to your passengers.
- Be the best pilot they've ever flown with.
- Pay attention to their physical needs.
- Never dismiss their fears.
- They rarely tell you everything, so ask.
- Body language is important.
- For unreasonable requests, cite safety as a reason to say no.
- Don't be a cowboy, it impresses no one.

—An old pilot

Chapter 13

CARE & FEEDING OF YOU

Bell 206L-1 LongRanger

The smoothest flying helicopter I ever took into the sky. A true pilot's machine.

Death is nature's way of saying watch your airspeed.

—*Anonymous*

AIDS: Aviation Induced Divorce Syndrome. You don't have to spend much time as a pilot before you'll hear this acronym. Unfortunately, there's an element of truth in the warning it offers. Perhaps more than any other job besides traveling salesperson, gossip columnist, or porn star, aviation can be tough on your relationships, marriages, and families. This is especially true when you're starting out. The path to becoming a pilot is littered with broken relationships and disappointed family members. You'll feel this tension after you arrive late, or not at all once again for the (fill in the blank) celebration.

One reason for the tension is where the jobs are located. Especially in the helicopter business, job postings will often ask you if you're willing to relocate. If you aren't prepared to strike your tent, and to move wherever the job is, often on an unaccompanied tour, operators will often find a pilot who is. As fellow aviator John Pountney said: "If you want the dream job on the other side of your home airfield, you'll probably have to get a job on the other side of the world first to get the required experience." Mr. Pountney flies Agusta Westwind aircraft in the UK, and this is the voice of experience.

My long ago posting in Alaska was one of my first assignments. I had to live in the Alaskan bush for an entire summer, leaving my wife and young daughter behind for nearly four months. It was tough, but at the time, it was a necessary ticket punch.

CHAPTER 13: CARE & FEEDING OF YOU

Here's how you might start: You'll do the hard work, sacrifice your time, attention, romance, fun, festivities, and a bucket load of cash, and you'll finally win your wings. Next, you'll apply for jobs. The natural vector is to be a flight instructor, to gain the hours that come with teaching others to fly. You'll move on from there. There's nothing wrong with instructing; it's an honorable position, and it can fill up your logbook faster than other methods, with the possible exception of military flying.

The first challenge you'll have is landing a "real job" and you may find that operators always want something just beyond what you have to offer: Maybe 1,500 logged hours instead of the 1,100 your logbook shows; or 300 hours of nighttime, instead of your 150; or 500 hours of turbine time when you've logged only 350. Operators and owners of aircraft are not evil or vindictive people. But in order to hire you to fly for them they need to be able to insure you. If an insurance provider won't cover you, forget it.

One point I must address, even though I'm hopeful you won't do it, is to pad your logbook. Years ago, I hired a pilot at the hospital, when the company requirement called for 3,000 hours total flight time. The fellow assured me that he had those hours, and he talked a good game, so I put him on the schedule. It was apparent very quickly that he had very little flight experience. His flying didn't reflect his alleged number of flight hours. Since

I had no way to verify his logbook, I hired him, restricting him to daytime flying for a while.

Early comments from the flight nurses made me uneasy. "He's a little rough with his landings," they'd say. Or "I wish he'd learn to navigate better," another one said. The concerns mounted. Shortly, the fellow moved on to another site, so his lack of polish and meager navigational skills ceased to be a problem for me. The lesson for you is, don't add flight hours you didn't fly. Experienced operators and check pilots can gauge pretty well how much experience you have.

When you're a rookie pilot, the beginning might be at the end of the road. Remote postings are the common path to your well-paying and respectable flying job. Sometimes those far-off jobs will be too strange and perilous to consider. My Panama tuna boat job was one of those.

There's another side to that scenario. Depending on what you want in either fixed or rotary wing aviation, those odd, quirky, *who knew?* jobs in exotic places can be the best ones you'll ever have. For example, it's a lot of fun dousing fires with a water bucket as I did in Alaska, or trimming trees with a buzz saw, as you've likely seen on YouTube videos, or flying an inter-island charter in a tropical location while building flight hours and working on your tan. Those positions may not pay much,

CHAPTER 13: CARE & FEEDING OF YOU

and in my opinion flying tourists all day can become boring, but the work is rewarding in its own way. As for your pay and bennies, they'll be all over the board. Flying tours on Kauai I made more money in tips than I did in salary at my first job! Strange but true.

About the blandishments of a flying life, there's a reason they're called *attractions*. It's because they can be awfully *attractive* at times. We've all heard about the temptations that will be available to you in certain specialties, the airlines, for example. There's a reason overnight stops are called layovers. For married pilots, either male or female, the layover world can offer one temptation after another, far from home, with prepaid beds available, and workmates equally lonely and willing to share their bed with you. Having children, especially young ones at home, will change your perspective, but you may be tempted anyway.

So, the advice I offer you is to avoid long-term relationships until the career is on solid ground, and until your life is stable. Granted, that may prove to be impossible. But rumors of divorce and marriage tension in the flying business are rampant, and those rumors are largely based on fact.

My own experience is a case in point. My ex followed me around from job to job, one aviation posting after another over the course of several years, until I established a *permanent* post flying at a hospital. Or as permanent as a flying job can be.

Because of the disruptions and moves from city to city, our relationship was strained already. We thought the hospital job would bring a bit of stability to our marriage. It didn't. My schedule was unpredictable; hours were long, despite so-called FAA mandated crew rest regs[16]; and I often brought the work home with me. It was all I talked about. Plus, shortly after I started flying at the hospital, the veteran lead pilot left and I was given his title, his responsibilities, and his pager! That meant wearing the electronic leash on what little time I had off, and the damned thing seemed to buzz precisely when I should have been at full attention with my wife and daughter.

Hospital flying, like any other charter flying, has another aggravation: In uncanny fashion, it seemed that if my wife and I scheduled a night out together, like clockwork, thirty minutes before shift change time the pager would erupt, and I'd fly away after calling her and canceling our date…again. We learned to not make plans for anything, and that's not a recipe for a happy home life. The message to you is that regardless of the kind of flying you'll do, on-call time can be a factor.

This brings me to another important point for you: Titles and positions can be one of the attractions, one of those bright shiny objects that you should ignore. When I became lead pilot and assumed the responsibility of running the hospital helicopter show, I felt I'd arrived at the pinnacle; that my dream job had

CHAPTER 13: CARE & FEEDING OF YOU

finally arrived. I reveled in the attention and respect I received because of my new title. But it turned out to be a typical middle management position, offering all the responsibilities with none of the authority.

After a few years of stamping out brush fires among the medical crew and pilots, refereeing dustups and disagreements between pilots and mechanics, herding combative cats day after day, the luster of the leadership position faded, and I gave up the managing job. Once I stepped down to a simple line pilot position, I felt better right away.

Next, consider the ephemeral nature, the spiritual, soulful part of flying. It's a fine idea to think outside the cockpit. You probably heard this question before you were five years old: "What do you want to be when you're big?" It's as if you must zero in on one job skill, and then live with it forever. This is hogtwaddle, of course. Even if your dream has always been to fly, there's nothing wrong with pursuing something else at the same time. For me, it was becoming an aviation writer. Over the years I've had several articles published in various trade and other commercial magazines. Don't be afraid to pursue other skills.

For years there've been rumors of a pilot shortage. I'm convinced that the shortage rumor originated among certain folks looking to boost salaries, or perhaps lower them, depending on whether the rumors originated with pilot groups or operators and aviation companies.

Regardless of what happens in the aviation industry, you should look out for yourself. Being dependent on a flying job to pay your rent forever may not be advisable, at least until you've achieved some longevity. I flew for a hospital for twenty years, and those were good, rewarding years, professionally, personally, and financially. But I heard of many fellow pilots who bounced from posting to posting, some for entire careers, without finding a permanent home.

Again, it depends on why you chose to fly. As with any other passion, there's a price tag attached to it. Let's discuss a few of the prices that accompany a career in aviation.

FOD is the acronym for Foreign Object Damage. Ordinarily, FOD is stuff that litters flight lines, such as maintenance detritus, discarded packaging, nuts, bolts, safety wire, and the like. Every flight line has Stop FOD warning signs, and many flight-line vehicles sport magnetic bars attached to their bumpers that suck up any FOD scattered around, at least the ferrous-metal type. There's a good reason for the caution about FOD: A loose $3.00 dzus fastener, or a misplaced $20.00 wrench can get vacuumed up and ruin a multi-million-dollar turboshaft engine.

But what about human FOD? What about things found on the flight line that cause damage to *your* health and wellbeing,

CHAPTER 13: CARE & FEEDING OF YOU

either acutely or chronically? If your goal is a lifetime aviation career, keep the following health-related items in mind.

The first one is aircraft-related hearing loss.[17] Especially while you're working around helicopters, wearing standard hearing protection might be enough for you, but only if you wear it consistently, and in some cases only if it's paired with other protection measures. Over my fifty-year career I sustained significant, bilateral hearing loss, despite having worn all the protection I could track down and use. As a fixed-wing pilot you may have an advantage here, but that assumption could be dangerous as well.

As a pilot, you won't often be exposed to the harmful effects of fuel and hydraulic mists, or airborne particulates, but there's a danger to you regardless of how little time you spend in those environments. Fuel handlers and mechanics work around those fluids all the time, and there's often little attention given to the health dangers that may cause them. Exposure to jet fuels and hydraulic fluids has been associated with such conditions as immune system dysfunctions, neural, reproductive, renal, and hepatic disorders.

The potential danger to you from recirculated air in aircraft cabins is dependent on the filters' efficiency, so there's likely little exposure to you as a pilot. But in certain situations—the cabin of a helicopter for example—where air is unfiltered you should consider wearing a mask, especially during certain exposures such as viral outbreaks.

On the topic of unhealthy air and human FOD, I'll just come out and say it. If you smoke cigarettes, you need to quit. You're asking for a lot of trouble, endangering your health, and (literally) burning up a ton of cash. No one smokes in a cockpit or near an aircraft anymore. Tobacco smoke and its residue gums up gauges and makes life difficult for mechanics.

Other health risks[18] for you as a pilot include a lack of exercise as you sit for long-duration flights and an unhealthful diet that might consist of vending machine fare. As a pilot, you may suffer disruptions in your circadian rhythms on long-haul or all-night flights. Chronic fatigue can accompany random flight scheduling, and reliance on over the counter (OTC) energy drugs or caffeine drinks to ward off fatigue can cause you long-term problems. Pilots may have exposure to common pathogens in the aircraft and cockpit as well.

I don't need to mention the use of illegal or recreational drugs. Pilots are made to pee in bottles all the time. If you're using drugs, you will be caught. By getting high, your dream will die.

Another risk, particularly in helicopter aviation, is back injury and low back strain.[18,19] I can attest that back problems are indeed a risk. In the middle of my career, after several episodes of back spasms, and many sleepless nights in pain,

CHAPTER 13: CARE & FEEDING OF YOU

I ruptured a disc in my back that required surgery. A physical therapist traced the problem to my time sitting in the cockpit. Fortunately, the operation on my back was successful, and I returned to the cockpit a few months later. It was an experience I don't wish to repeat. It was painful, and the rehab was tedious. Plus, it disrupted the crew schedule and could have grounded me permanently. So, I recommend that you find a daily exercise regimen for your back health and make it part of your routine. This is especially true if you fly helicopters where there's typically no autopilot, no way to get up and stretch during a flight, and no co-pilot to hand over the controls to.

Along with the above health-related items, you need to consider the stress involved in your annual flight physical. In order to keep flying you must pass this test every year, or more often, until you retire. Give yourself every chance to pass it. Stop smoking, exercise, eat a decent diet, get plenty of sleep, and don't use energy drinks and such.

Another stressor is that there may be a penalty for you if you call in sick too often, disrupting a company flight schedule. Also, you'll be hesitant to complain about long work hours, or the physical toll of flying, because other people don't want to hear it. There are other risks to your health and welfare in a flying life—crashing comes to mind—but if you take standard precautions, use a little common sense, and the tools I offer you in this book, there's no reason you can't stay in the air a lot longer than I did.

Lessons:

- You may have to be selfish. Capturing your dream to fly is worth it.
- Don't grovel, but don't be afraid to say no. Keep your head up.
- Check with the insurance provider about logged hours required.
- As difficult as it might be, don't be afraid to confront a cowboy pilot. You're flying an aircraft they've been flying, and your career could be on the line.
- Never pad your logbook. Veteran employers can sense your experience or lack of it.
- If you can't stay single, look for another pilot. He/She will understand better than a non-flyer.
- Have another useful skill to fall back on.
- No smoking.
- Wear hearing protection.
- No drugs.
- Sit up straight.
- Get plenty of sleep and exercise.
- Always pick up FOD.

—*An old pilot*

Chapter 14

CARE & FEEDING OF YOUR CREW
Crew Resource Management

Kaloa Outrigger Canoe Club off Kauai

Author's wife, in the boat's 4th position. My wahine was about to win the 2005 PoiPu Challenge, a 10-mile race.

(CRM) prevents aviation mishaps. Period. Introduced to airline cockpits many years ago, Cockpit Resource Management CRM was soon altered to Crew Resource Management[20] to reflect the roles of the entire crew in aviation safety. The short version of what CRM does is this: It recognizes all members of the flight crew as agents of safety, encouraging their input and insight regardless of rank or pay grade. Just as with the individual paddlers in the outrigger canoe above, every piece of data, and every idea or bit of advice is important to the safety and success of the operation. CRM removed the old and caustic "captain knows best" attitude that once reigned in aircraft cockpits, replacing it with the understanding that all crewmembers have a stake in safe operations and that their valuable resources must be used.

> See it, Say it, Fix it!
> —*CRM Mantra*

When it was introduced, CRM had an immediate positive impact on safety in the FAR Part 121 flying business. These days an airline accident is a rare occurrence. There are several reasons for the safety record, including better equipment, extensive radar coverage, better training for crews, better airport infrastructure, more sophisticated simulators, and more FAA oversight. But one of the biggest reasons airline flying is safer is CRM.

CHAPTER 14: CARE AND FEEDING OF YOUR CREW

Used correctly and consistently, Crew Resource Management will help prolong your career, make your flying more enjoyable, and relatively free of stress and strain from worry about basic threats to your aircraft and longevity, and from weather and aircraft malfunctions. Minimizing unsafe elements from your flying allows you to better enjoy what you're doing, makes you more productive, enhances your reputation as a safe pilot, and gives you more bandwidth to deal with emergencies or challenges. CRM isn't a get-out-of-jail-free card. It's the ticket to a long rewarding—and safe—career in the sky. It can also be employed in a single-pilot cockpit, without difficulty.

Before I get to the details of CRM, I'll give a shout out to Randy Mains, a fellow aviator who introduced me to CRM, and who teaches the CRM program in a train-the-trainer capacity.[24] If you have an interest in learning about CRM, and/or becoming an instructor in its implementation for your company or site, Randy's contact info follows at the end of this chapter and in the bibliography.

Here's the basic outline of Crew Resource Management and a few of its applications. Following each notation is an antidote for change, and an example of an accident or situation CRM could have prevented. This is an abbreviated version of CRM.

9 HAZARDOUS ATTITUDES: 9 ANTIDOTES: 9 EXAMPLES:

Note: We all have some of these. It's called being human.

1. **Anti-Authority:** "Don't tell me what to do! The rules don't apply to me."
   Antidote: Follow the rules. They apply to everyone.
   Example: See Chapter 3 Stretching the Rules.

2. **Impulsive Attitude:** "Do something! Fast!"
   Antidote: Slow down. Give it some thought.
   Example: "Let's go before the weather closes in!"

3. **Invulnerability:** "It can't happen to me."
   Antidote: Realization that it can happen to you
   Example: Capt. Smith of RMS Titanic, after forty years at sea.

4. **"Macho" can-do attitude.** Letting our ego fly the aircraft.
   Antidote: Avoid taking risks just to impress people.
   Example: My attempt to lift the heavy gun in Vietnam. (Chapter 11)

5. **Resignation:** "What's the use?"
   Antidote: It's not about luck; it's your actions that matter.

CHAPTER 14: CARE AND FEEDING OF YOUR CREW

Example: Capt. Sullivan in The High & The Mighty

6. **Refusing to challenge experts:** Assuming the old dude is right. The mirror image of this is assuming expertise that we don't have.
   Antidote: Speak up anyway.
   Example: The crew of Korean Airlines Flight 801 on Guam, 1997

7. **Press-on-itis:** Also called Get-home-itis.
   Antidote: Better late than never.
   Example: Too many to mention. We've all done this.

8. **Risky shift, or Groupthink:** Going along to make nice.
   Antidote: Recognize it and step outside the group.
   Example: NW Airlines 6231 12/1/1974.
   (Fascinating NTSB report!)

9. **Anchoring bias:** Weather is better than crap, so let's go!
   Antidote: A good dose of objectivity.
   Example: Lear 35 crash Teterboro NJ, May 2017.

THE ERROR CHAIN
Break the chain—Stop the accident

Every accident offers clues to its cause and possible prevention. Identifying those clues beforehand, like breaking a link in a chain, can eliminate the chance of an accident. It's not possible to eliminate all risk from aviation. But it is possible to identify opportunities for breaking chains that may lead to an accident. Here are the common links to look out for:

1. <u>**Ambiguity:**</u> When two sources of information don't agree. Clarification is always a good thing. Never be afraid or embarrassed to ask. There's no such thing as a stupid question.
2. <u>**Fixation/Preoccupation:**</u> Identify the *real* problem, and delegate roles. Read the account of Eastern Airlines flight 401 from December 1972. Focusing on a burned out fifty-cent light bulb led to the loss of 101 lives, and a $40 million L-1011.

CHAPTER 14: CARE AND FEEDING OF YOUR CREW

3. <u>Confusion:</u> Always be five miles ahead of the aircraft. One solution for confusion is simple. Slow down.
4. **No one flying the aircraft:** As a pilot, you must never become a passenger. This is similar to the hazardous attitude of resignation. There's always something you can do as a pilot.
5. **No one looking out the window:** In any crew situation it should be protocol for someone to be looking outside at all times. Note: Automated cockpit systems can compound this problem.

The CRM concept is applicable in any aviation scenario, whether in a single-pilot situation or a crewed aircraft setting. The following are a few of the examples of times when CRM worked, and my crew and I stayed safe to fly another day.

1. <u>Anti-Authority:</u> Tom Kearsley, a fellow pilot in Vietnam, had an anti-authority attitude. His posture was doubly dangerous because he was the company instructor pilot.
2. <u>Impulsive Attitude:</u> One afternoon as a thunderstorm approached, I took off in the hospital helicopter to put it in the hangar. Our hangar was located in the direction of the storm. I took off anyway, assuming potential hail and wind damage could be a worse scenario. Worse than flying in a thunderstorm?

3. **Invulnerability:** Jim, my colleague on Kauai, died in a helicopter crash because he didn't believe it could happen to him.
4. **"Macho" or Can-do attitude:** My assumption that I could sling-load the heavy gun in Vietnam stemmed from this attitude.
5. **Resignation:** Capt. Sullivan in The High and the Mighty.
6. **Refusing to challenge experts:** Here's what Randy Mains has to say about this hazardous attitude:

    When I flew as a captain with a rookie pilot I'd ask them this question: "Who is the most dangerous person in the cockpit today?" Invariably my young copilot would sheepishly raise their hand and say they were. I'd correct them by saying "No, I am, because you don't think I can make a mistake, and I guarantee you I can and perhaps will. That's why, if you see something you don't like or makes you uncomfortable, I want you to please bring it up."

7. **Get-home-itis:** An air medical accident in the mountains of Colorado several years ago revealed that the pilot accepted the flight very close to his shift change time. When he arrived at the site of the injured climber, there was no safe place to land. EMTs told

him they'd carry the victim downslope where he could be placed in the helicopter, but it would take at least an hour. To expedite the operation, the pilot tried to land closer. His rotor blades hit a rock wall. He crashed, killing himself and two flight crewmembers.

8. **Risky shift, or Groupthink:** Despite more than 50,000 hours collective flight time in the cockpit, Northwest Airlines flight 6231[25] crashed anyway. It was December 1974, in the days of flight engineers, and all three pilots in the cockpit mistook a pending stall for Mach buffet, the warning that the aircraft was about to break the sound barrier! (This is the most fascinating NTSB report I ever read. I encourage you to look it over, it contains every item on the preceding list of things to avoid.)

9. **Anchoring bias:** A Learjet crash at Teterboro, NJ resulted from the pilot's poor assessment of crosswind conditions, and his eroding airspeed in a turn. Winds had been somewhat weaker earlier that day, and he assumed the landing would be easier.

An addendum to CRM and its application: Many studies have shown that other factors determine safe operations, such things as cultural mores, physiological status, age, life events both positive and negative, and also gender. It may be speculation, but it's possible that, despite male domination of aviation, women may be better suited to it in terms of safe operations.

Scanning the various attitudes and behaviors addressed by CRM, it's easier to assign the negative traits, for example anti-authority, invulnerability, and macho attitude, to men over women. Not that women are immune to many of those attitudes and behaviors; some of them are simply attributes of being human. But women seem to be less susceptible to unsafe attitudes, and they've been acculturated, at least in our society, toward a more other-oriented mentality, a more CRM-aware methodology. Testosterone spikes may be more dangerous than fuel exhaustion or a chip light.

A final note on a new training and evaluation method known as EBT, or Evidence Based Training. EBT appears to be the future of not only training but of checkrides as well. As an old, retired pilot, I have little familiarity with EBT. The new methodology was introduced only in 2013, after I retired from flying, and is just now appearing in classrooms and cockpits as a safety and evaluation tool. It isn't meant to replace, but to compliment CRM techniques, and is basically a reworking of training methods, focusing on core competencies, moving away from the 1960s approach to it, bringing training and eval into the 21st century.

CHAPTER 14: CARE AND FEEDING OF YOUR CREW

Years ago, when I flew at the hospital, the medical staff was learning a new approach to medical care and intervention called Evidence Based Medicine. That new approach moved medical care out of laboratories and classrooms, away from the sanitized, hypothetical method of patient care—from here's what *should* work, according to the gurus, because it's what we've always done before—to observing which protocols, drugs, and procedures work with actual patients, in actual hospital settings, and using that hard data instead. The difference in patient outcomes has been remarkable.

My understanding of EBT is that flight trainers and check airmen are adopting it in their cockpits because it's moving away from hypothetical to real-world situations, thus producing better outcomes for pilots.

I've included a link in the resources section and the bibliography for more information about EBT. My guess is that, unless you're familiar with it already, EBT will be part of your curriculum at some point in your flying career. And that's a very good thing.

Chapter 15

CARE & FEEDING OF YOUR CAREER

CH-47D Chinook

September 21, 2000. I'd just landed this Chinook after taking my kid brother, an Army recruiter, for a spin. It was the last time I flew a military helicopter

As I mentioned in a previous chapter, regardless of which category of aircraft you're flying, the industry is very small, and the rumor mill is extremely efficient, especially these days with social media and pilot forums. Because aviation, especially in the airlines, is so safe today the slightest hiccup focuses attention on the crew. Every passenger owns a hand-held, movie studio/broadcast booth in their cell phones these days, so as a pilot you'll be under more scrutiny than ever. Here are a few ways to preserve your anonymity, which is what you want to do, so you can enjoy a long and happy, stress-free and accident-free life in the cockpit.

First, I'll list a few things you really *don't* want to do. For starters, you don't want to mislead a potential employer about logged hours, aircraft flown, or your certifications. It's easy these days to reproduce a license, a medical certificate, or indeed any kind of document you may wish to copy. It's equally easy to check for their veracity. If you plagiarize a certificate, and then get caught, which you inevitably will, your flying career could be over. Some of this advice may seem simplistic, but there are people who attempt such dishonesties just to land a flying job. Here's an example from my good friend and fellow author Randy Mains:

> I was hired to fly for an air medical program in San Diego… to replace a pilot who had been fired for changing the date on his medical certificate, because he'd forgotten to renew it. Besides losing his job, he'd committed a felony according to the FAA.

CHAPTER 15: CARE & FEEDING OF YOUR CAREER

If you damage an aircraft, especially in the early part of your career, 'fess up, make a commitment to fly better, and put it behind you. There are a number of pilots out there who have damaged aircraft. Though it's embarrassing and expensive, and it can be dangerous or even fatal of course, the true test to you will be in your recovery from the incident, both physically and mentally. As odd as it may sound, a close call, or a slightly pranged aircraft could be the best lesson you'll ever get.

As for FAA violations, the best way for you to avoid them is to know the regulations, and the aircraft and its operation, including any service bulletins (SB) and airworthiness directives (AD)[21] in place for the machine you're flying. Knowing the rules for every regime you encounter and having a clear knowledge of what airspace you're flying in can keep you out of trouble.

You may hear from others that the Federal Aviation Administration (FAA) and Air Traffic Control (ATC) are gunning for pilots, and constantly looking for ways to violate you. In my fifty years in the cockpit, I had no such experience. On the contrary, I found ATC professionals to be gracious with their assistance, especially while handling rookie pilots, and not at all eager to call out a pilot's infractions. That said, an egregious violation, such as ignoring a radio directive, or entering restricted airspace will likely get you more than a slap on the wrist.

If you think you've inadvertently entered a restricted area, missed an ATC instruction, or endangered another pilot and their aircraft in some actionable way, submit the standard form under the NASA Aviation Safety Reporting System (ASRS). It's a good idea to keep a few of these forms in your flight bag. You can submit them electronically, but not by email for security reasons. They're like your insurance policy if you're unsure if your actions will bring an FAA inspector to your doorstep.

This is a good place to mention visits from FAA personnel. As a pilot, you may find these events tense and filled with anxiety. Sometime in your career you'll get "ramped." Representatives of the federal aviation administration (FAA) will meet you either on the flight line or at your office. They'll ask to see your flying certificate, your medical clearance, and also the aircraft flight and maintenance logbooks.

The best way to approach getting "ramped" is to be honest, show the requested paperwork, and cooperate fully. Those FAA individuals are doing an important job, and as I mentioned above, they're not set on finding fault. Unless the FAA finds some egregious violation or paperwork lapse, the ramp check will last a very short time and you'll be back in the air.

Another piece of advice comes from a colleague, Colten Christopher Fronk:

> One very important thing I learned the hard way is you need Aircraft Owner's and Pilot's Association, (AOPA)'s Pilot Protection Program.[22] You may try to do everything

right, but there is that one day you unexpectedly need it, and it's like insurance. If you don't have it beforehand it doesn't help you.

The insurance plan Mr. Fronk refers to is AOPA's Pilot Protection Service, which offers advice and legal counsel to members.

Indeed, membership in AOPA has many benefits, whether you fly commercially or not. The AOPA hasn't given me a nickel for adding this blurb, but the organization does offer a lot, so I encourage pilots to look into it.

A few other trade organizations you may consider:
1. Professional Pilots Association (PPA)
2. For women pilots The Ninety-Nines
3. Airline pilots have Airline Pilots Association, (ALPA)
4. Combat Helicopter Pilots Association, (CHPA)
5. AOPA's affiliation with Helicopter Association International, (HAI)
6. Alpha Eta Rho: Coed international professional college aviation fraternity

Some of these groups require qualifications, for example, flight time in combat to belong to CHPA. Many are open to new members, dues are reasonable, and membership comes with useful resources that will help or enhance your career. Some of them list scholarships available to aspiring pilots. (I itemize a few of these scholarship opportunities in the resources section of the book)

Another way to help yourself as a pilot is to be your own safety advocate. That is, never give less than 100% in the cockpit, don't be afraid to say no if you think an operation is unsafe, and don't hesitate to pass on an assignment you feel is beyond your capability. Here's some advice on that from Stephen Walton, a pilot for a major U.S. airline:

THE DAYNO RESPONSE

Coming up, flying Part 91 freight was (like) the Wild West. I always had $1000 in traveler's checks in my back pocket. The reason for that was, when starting out in those low-ranking jobs, you will be asked to compromise one thing or another. You make your decisions as you go, but there may be a day when you say, "Dayno." In other words, "Dayno freaking way I'm gonna do that." That's when you pick up your stuff, and head for the door.

With $1000 in your back pocket, you can find shelter, and start home. Bottom line—not always appreciated by newbies—is, "You have to be alive to spend it." You also have to be alive to starve to death. Credit cards take the place of traveler's checks these days, but you get the idea. Commitment is having no alternatives.

CHAPTER 15: CARE & FEEDING OF YOUR CAREER

Thanks for this pearl of wisdom Captain Walton. "Dayno" way I was leaving it out. As a rookie pilot, you're not trying to impress anyone. You're trying to gain experience, and that effort will pay dividends. In addition to building hours in the cockpit, you'll be cementing your reputation as a safe, knowledgeable, conscientious, and reliable pilot. That's as good as gold in the aviation industry.

Nothing will shorten your flying career faster than showing off and putting an aircraft in the dirt. I'm now retired after fifty years in the sky, so I can discuss this freely. After 12,500 hours of incident and accident-free flying, I can tell you that if you respect yourself and your aircraft, the likelihood that your career will match mine for safety is quite high. One of the reasons I flew safely all those years was that I understood how quickly I could lose my spotless record. I flew—every day—with the intention of maintaining it. In other words, my safety record didn't happen by accident.

JOB PREP: RÉSUMÉS/INTERVIEWS/TRAINING CLASS

Here are basic things you should keep in mind once you obtain proper certification, and are qualified for your dream job, or at least a position with a company that's hiring. First of all, as I mentioned earlier, regardless of what the job market looks like at this point, don't assume it will stay this way. The aviation industry is volatile, and especially in the airline business, hiring and furloughs seem to happen whenever the wind changes direction.

But let's assume the industry is hiring pilots, you're qualified for the position you want, and you need advice on how to leave the Director of Operations' (DO) office with a job offer. Here are a few things to remember.

RÉSUMÉS

Before anything else, craft a quality résumé. Make it one page. Your résumé needs to be on clean, crisp, white paper, with a standard font like Times New Roman. If the company you're applying to has a style or a format, or a different application method, by all means pay attention to that. Your résumé represents you to a total stranger, so it needs to tell them you're someone they'd hire to represent their company. Despite its outward appearances of fantasy, and often-exotic advertising, aviation can be a fairly stuffy, conservative endeavor, especially in the airlines. Flashy paperwork, and odd, atypical or "cutesy" approaches to a position won't work. That bright-red paper with the 45 font lettering will indeed attract attention, and then it will go directly into the circular file. Outliers need not apply, in other words.

A DO or chief pilot will look for certain things in a

CHAPTER 15: CARE & FEEDING OF YOUR CAREER

potential pilot's résumé besides basic qualifications, which any pilot must have. She will look for attention to detail: Did the applicant follow directions? Did she or he use the application format listed on the company website? Is the flight qualification section filled out as required? Does the total time add up? Are there gaps and missing blocks that raise questions? Flying is, after all, a business that demands following directions, so show you can do that.

Here are a few items to remember that might automatically disqualify you, things that real pilot applicants have done:

1. Don't send your résumé to a DO or chief pilot who's retired or has left the company. Find out who the proper person is and send it to them.
2. Don't embarrass yourself by sending it in the wrong fashion, through snail-mail instead of on-line, for example. One pilot shamed herself by express packaging her paperwork via FedEx, when applying to fly for UPS!
3. Don't barge into the DO's office insisting on hand carrying the résumé. Enthusiasm has its place, but so does basic courtesy.
4. Don't include a cover letter unless asked for one.
5. Don't make a two-page résumé, just one page. If you have to use smaller fonts to cover everything, do that instead.

6. Do list credentials you've earned, even if you haven't used them for a while. And use the proper terminology. You're a certificated flight instructor, not certified. That's a grocery item.

A cleaner résumé is better. Here's a suggested format:
1. Personal stats: Name, address, phone number, email address, job applying for. If your street address is variable, list one where you can expect to receive mail.
2. Make sure your cell phone number is correct. New carriers & SIM cards can change these.
3. Flight credentials: What you've flown and for who.
4. Certifications: Use ASEL, AMEL, ATP etc. plus FAA medical. Listing a Class 1 medical is better, even if it's not needed.
5. Flight times: Itemize by Total Time, PIC/SIC, turbojet, night, IFR, Sim time etc. These times must tally, and don't round the numbers. Make them exact. Expect a DO or chief pilot to add them up. There could be nasty surprises or embarrassing questions at the interview if they don't match.
6. Don't list cross-country time, as it's irrelevant to your qualifications.
7. Education obtained: Degree(s), years attended, academic awards or achievements.

CHAPTER 15: CARE & FEEDING OF YOUR CAREER

8. Recent employment history: Past ten years suggested.
9. Accomplishments: Any awards, decorations, writing, relevant flying goals achieved. If in doubt add them, unless it makes the résumé more than one page.
10. Don't leave blank spaces. If there's nothing to add, use N/A.

A DO or chief pilot will likely Google you, so Google yourself first. Then Google the person you're applying to. They'll check up on you, so check up on them. You may find things in your own file that you'll be asked to explain, and you'll learn things about possible employers as well, things that may help in your interview.

Something else to check is your driving record. If you have a black mark on your driver's permit, a DUI for instance, it will appear in a background check. You'll want to address that, pay any outstanding fines, clear up speed bumps etc., or petition for removal of certain items. One fellow received a DUI on the way home from celebrating his CFI check ride, and it took him two years to get past it. If you do your own background check, you won't be asked questions about things of which you may not be aware. It's possible to get paranoid about this process, but it's always better to be fully prepared, and to be fully transparent as well. Employers don't like nasty surprises, and they appreciate honesty.

Finally, if you have any doubts about your résumé, have an employed professional pilot, someone you trust, look it over and make comments, or pay a professional résumé prep company. And if the DO asks for copies of your certificates, don't forget to copy both sides, and double check that nothing is expired.

THE INTERVIEW

When you're asked to come in for an interview, you may be halfway to a job, but there's still work to do. Study up on the company, the website, the staff, and know as much as you can about them before you go. If you know anyone who works for the company, ask them every question you can think of. Read aviation industry magazines and newsletters so you can be conversant with current issues in the business.

Dress like someone you'd hire if they came to you for a job. Remember, there's no second chance to make a first impression, so dress conservatively, understated, and as you'd expect if you were on the other side of the hiring desk. Here's a tip: Airlines hire captains, not first officers (FOs). The DO needs to see you as a pilot who can do the job someday from the left seat, not a permanent right-seater.

Basics count: Be on time, or better yet early. Smile. Look them in the eye. A firm handshake is good. One colleague said to make the interview "like a three-day airline trip, thinking about every issue, problem, challenge, sign, and eventuality you can come up with, and then think of a solution for each one." Think about customer issues, crew problems, mechanical breakdowns, weather delays, in-flight emergencies, scheduling changes, whatever comes to mind. Fly a few routes and throw in problems along the way. Put yourself in the job, in other words, and you'll interview better.

If the interviewer asks a question you didn't expect, or that may embarrass you, take time to respond. Don't lie about something, ever. If there's a discrepancy in your flight times, for example, thank them for finding it, and say you'll check your records.

Despite all the firewalls, legal protections, and systemic barriers against discrimination, a company can still find a reason to turn you down. Try to fit in without sacrificing your dignity. And of course, though you may be desperate for the work, if an interviewer crosses a line into harassment, be prepared to walk away.

Be as familiar as you can be with the regulations. Study up on FAR Parts 1, 61, 91, 135, and any others that may apply. Know the Airman's Information Manual, (AIM). Be familiar with the company route structure, and the aircraft used.

Lastly, if you're offered a job and asked when you can start, don't throw a current employer under the rug. Aviation is a very small, quite intimate business, and courtesy is still appreciated. Say you can start in two weeks, the standard response, and that will be fine.

I've included a sampling of interview-related books in the bibliography.

TRAINING CLASS

You've sent in your résumé, been called for an interview, and then offered a flying job with XYZ Airline. The hiring letter indicates what class you'll be part of, when it starts, and where to report. Here are a few tips that will get you through the classes and started on your long-dreamt-of career with the airlines.

Make sure your paperwork is in order and is gathered in an orderly, easy-to-access system. If there are discrepancies or errors, fix them right away.

Every airline has a dress code. Find out what it is, and follow it. As I wrote before, the airlines can be a bit stuffy. Don't show up in blue jeans or overly casual clothes.

If you know what equipment you'll be flying, track down the Aircraft Operating Manual (AFM) and study it. Get a copy of the airline's call-outs, standard operating procedures, (SOPs), FAA operations specifications, (Op-Specs), aircraft systems manual, and the normal checklist for the aircraft. If there's a quick reference handbook, (QRH) study it well. This handy guide usually has so called "memory items," procedures that must be done by rote, such as responses to engine fires, cabin decompression etc.

Even if the cost is high, get as much flight time as possible, and immerse yourself in the tough part of it. Don't just cut holes in the sky. Practice crosswind landings, radio procedures, every instrument approach you might encounter, especially ILS and GPS/RNAV, and go through emergency procedures for whatever aircraft you're flying.

Here's a tip: Fly approaches at a much higher airspeed than you're used to, so you're more comfortable in a faster environment. Doing this helps improve your instrument scan.

If you can find one, and it fits in your budget—or even if it doesn't—pay for simulator time, and make the most of it. Acquiring a type rating may be advisable as well. Though not cheap, being typed in the aircraft that the airline uses will be a real plus.

Another tip: Dress warmly for sim sessions. Simulator rooms are kept pretty chilly to pamper all the computerized stuff, and those rooms tend to be cold.

For the time you're in training, usually four to six weeks depending on the airline, you may have family issues, friends wanting to see you and party, or other personal challenges. As much as possible, put those aside, and focus solely on your training.

Try to sleep as well as you can. Don't eat junk from the school vending machines, but healthy, wholesome food. Avoid too much alcohol consumption. (Avoiding booze altogether is a better idea.) And of course, forget the weed, and any other non-authorized and un-prescribed drugs. Illicit drug use is the quickest way to throw your flying career in the crapper.

Between classes, exercise and relax as much as you can. Don't abandon your previous life completely, watch your favorite shows, and eat like you do at home. Call friends to share what's going on.

Last, take advantage of a study group if one is offered. Remember, you've been hired by the airline, so you're not in competition with other trainees. Every student brings something to the room, and the best way to learn is to be open to your own limits. When you fly the simulator, you'll be in the box with another student. Use that time to its fullest. Challenge each other, and don't be afraid to ask for help. There are no dumb questions.

CHAPTER 15: CARE & FEEDING OF YOUR CAREER

Lessons:
- Don't piss people off.
- The FAA is not out to get you.
- In aviation, knowledge = insurance. Stock up.
- Be a professional. It may cost you, but professionalism is more than worth it.
- Make the résumé one page.
- You're not certified; you're certificated.
- Dress as a professional for the interview.
- Make your résumé shine and make it accurate.
- Aviation is a conservative business, so try to fit in without sacrificing your dignity.
- The airlines hire captains, not FOs.

—An old pilot

Chapter 16

CONFESSIONS, STORIES & VOICES OF EXPERIENCE

> Aviation in itself is not inherently dangerous. But to an even greater degree than the sea, it is terribly unforgiving of any carelessness, incapacity or neglect.

You had one job...

Any decision made for convenience is probably the wrong one.
—*Jake Molter*

In this chapter I'll discuss the various ways of flying safely and how you can complete your aviation career with zero black marks. Using war stories from colleagues, I'll show how easy it can be to first enter into the error chain that can lead you, especially as a newer pilot, into an overwhelming situation. I also show how you can identify the chain of events that leads to a possible accident, and how to break that chain before it breaks you.

It's too easy to point fingers and to rush to judgment when a crash occurs. After an aviation mishap, the media are filled with speculation about what caused it. In many cases, the immediate assumption is that pilot error played a part in the crash. This chapter will hopefully show you how to stay out of the news, or out of trees as the case may be.

I don't believe in accidents. Every mishap has an explanation, something overlooked that allowed it to propagate and bloom. Using examples from colleagues who have graciously allowed me to include their stories here, I'll present you with some of the faulty decisions—my own included—that could have led to a crash. I'll begin with my tale of a night flight in fog that had all the ingredients for a typical air medical helicopter accident. Here's what happened:

I'd left the hospital helipad at 11 p.m. on a balmy November night to rescue a heart attack victim. Local emergency medical

CHAPTER 16: CONFESSIONS, STORIES & VOICES OF EXPERIENCE

technicians (EMTs) had called for our helicopter to meet them at the victim's farmhouse, twenty-five miles away. Weather was ceiling and visibility unlimited (CAVU), with a temperature-dew point spread of four degrees.

Since it would be just a fifteen-minute flight, I assumed the mission would be easy, and that I'd be back to the hospital in an hour or less. I leveled off, cleaned up the cockpit, and flew along fat, dumb, and happy, another routine flight.

Well... It turned out to be one of the longest nights of my career.

I landed at the victim's farmhouse, and the nurses zipped inside to tend to their patient.

I stayed with the aircraft, assuming they'd be back very soon, and that we'd load the patient aboard, and quickly fly him away. Shortly after I landed, the slight breeze died and the air became utterly still. After thirty minutes, with no medical patient, I looked to the west. A tall radio tower that I'd passed on the way to the scene was no longer visible. Its lights had vanished. At first, I thought they'd gone out, that after midnight those lights automatically extinguished or something... That was not the reason I couldn't see them.

After I'd been on the ground an hour, still with no patient to fly, I felt a chill mist in the air. Looking straight up I saw that the stars had disappeared. Fog was forming. I walked into the house, where the flight nurses were still bent over the old farmer, cardiopulmonary resuscitation (CPR) in progress. There were medical supplies scattered around on the floor and no sign that the medical crew was ready to leave.

I beckoned to one of my crew, telling him that the weather was closing in. He assured me they'd be back to the helicopter shortly, so I returned to the aircraft.

Another half hour went by. Finally, the patient and my crew came out and we loaded the man inside. I buttoned up the aircraft, started the engine, and took off at 1 a.m., hoping visibility wasn't as bad as it appeared to be from the ground.

It was worse. As I leveled off at 400 feet, dense billows of fog rolled past the aircraft. I eased the airspeed back to sixty knots, fifty, then forty.

At one point I slowed a bit too much, and the airspeed needle dropped below thirty knots, bouncing close to zero. If the needle had gone to zero and stayed there, I wouldn't know if I was moving forward, sideways, or backward. Luckily, the needle climbed back to thirty knots, showing I had forward airspeed.

An old aviation adage says that if it's bad on the ground it will only get worse in the air. Well, things got worse pretty quickly. When the crew loaded the patient that night, they'd inadvertently banged the patient cot against the defrost knob, jamming it tight.

CHAPTER 16: CONFESSIONS, STORIES & VOICES OF EXPERIENCE

Then, as they pumped the man's chest, their sweaty exertions inside the cabin caused the windows of the aircraft to steam up. I tried cranking the defog valve open, but the knob wouldn't budge. So, I kicked the aircraft out of trim and opened the side vent at my right shoulder to get some fresh air into the cabin. Nearly hovering along, crabbing sideways in the murky night, I peered ahead hoping to break out and see something I recognized.

Then I remembered the radio tower. It was somewhere between me and the hospital, somewhere close by. I had no idea where, nor did I know where its massive guy wires were. I continued with the heading I thought would keep me clear, staring ahead, looking for red lights in the fog.

The nearby ATC facility was closed up for the night, so radar wasn't available. I was 400 feet off the ground, nearly hovering from farm light to farm light, with the medical team doing CPR on the patient beside me, and oblivious to the danger they were in.

After what seemed an eternity, the hazy lights of Iowa City shimmered in the fog ahead. I steered toward the hospital, landed, and vowed to never, ever put myself in that position again. I envisioned the subsequent reports of the crash, and the fog, and the loss of control, and the inevitable finger pointing and shaking heads as yet another air medical helicopter crashed, with four fatalities. People talk about their lives flashing in front of them. I could see the headlines with my name in them.

My alternatives that night were limited, but they were available, if only I'd used them. I could have left the team with the patient, insisting that they use the ground ambulance instead, and flown home. I could have climbed and radioed a distress call to any open air traffic control (ATC) resource. I could have landed right away when I noticed the extent of the fog. In other words, I had options; I chose not to use them.

At the time, I was a member of the Iowa National Guard, assigned as one of the unit's instrument flight examiners. I had many hours of weather time, so the fog itself didn't elicit panic, or distract me from the immediate task of flying the aircraft. Loss of control can happen within thirty seconds of inadvertent entry into instrument meteorological conditions (IMC). Pilots lacking the skills and confidence to fly on instruments are naturally more vulnerable.

That was not a factor for me. But the helicopter I was flying that night wasn't equipped for instrument flight. It had a single artificial horizon, a crude turn and bank indicator, one generator that, fortunately, didn't fail, and no GPS or night vision equipment like many cockpits have now. So, the lack of proper navigation equipment in that helicopter added to my burden. But my instrument flying skills were excellent.

CHAPTER 16: CONFESSIONS, STORIES & VOICES OF EXPERIENCE

The recent crash that killed Kobe Bryant and eight other people is instructive.[23] The pilot held an instrument instructor rating; the aircraft was equipped for IFR operations; and though the aircraft was too low to use it, the IFR/ATC system was available to him.

While the crash was tragic, and again without tendering judgment, that was not an accident. In other words, it didn't have to happen. The error chain for it is clear: Weather, plus pressure to fly, plus low skill/currency in instrument flight techniques, plus rising terrain, *equaled* a deadly crash. My own night in the fog could have had the same result, so I don't disparage the pilot of that Sikorsky.

I was fortunate that foggy night. After landing, I literally kissed the helipad. The error chain in my flight in the fog was, No. 1, assuming that weather would hold, No. 2, a false belief that the medical team would expedite with the patient, No. 3, my haste with pre-takeoff preparations, No. 4, a takeoff with no weather report, and No. 5, a lack of orientation to obstacles in my flight path...

What I've just written is my own NTSB accident report. It describes the error chain I should have broken that night but did not. It's also why I don't judge other pilots' decisions, because in every accident report I've read—and I've read a lot of them—I nod my head, knowing that I'd once been in that cockpit.

Here's the final part of this frightening tale of my flight in the fog, the conclusion that put it all in even sharper focus: When we brought the old farmer into the emergency room, he was immediately pronounced dead. I'd endangered myself and my team for nothing.

Next, a story of a US Coast Guard helicopter aircrew at night over the Atlantic Ocean, a concrete example of the value of Crew Resource Management, (CRM), a safety initiative I discuss in the next chapter. Commander Elizabeth Booker's story also shows how important it is to trust your instruments. Here's Cmdr. Liz Booker:

Sometimes the most impactful lessons are delivered on the most benign flights.

I was at about 1200 hours (logged) in the H65 Dolphin helicopter on a routine night law enforcement patrol between Miami and Bimini, where drug-runners and migrant smugglers often make their last leg to US soil. I was at the top of my game—confident, proficient, flying thirty to fifty hours a month, two and a half hours at a time. I'd had plenty of challenging offshore hoists and was the best I'd ever be at ship landings, so the monotony of another zigzag over familiar waters was nothing to worry about.

CHAPTER 16: CONFESSIONS, STORIES & VOICES OF EXPERIENCE

My co-pilot, Rob, wasn't a nugget (rookie) anymore, but he wasn't a qualified aircraft commander yet, either. We'd flown together several times and were playful and friendly—he called me Beth to annoy me, so I called him Bobby to annoy him. We were in the middle of our patrol against a steady twenty-five to thirty knot headwind, with almost no illumination, when our mechanic spotted a flashing white light below in the water. As a Coast Guard crew, we're always on the lookout for mariners in distress. A white light could be anything . . . a life-jacket marker, a drug drop . . . we turned the aircraft around, briefed, and set up for a standard instrument approach to a fifty-foot hover into the wind. We decided I'd fly the approach and put the flashing light down the left side of the aircraft for Bobby to take a look.

Everything went smoothly on approach. Following procedures, Bobby stayed on the instruments with me until I was in a stable taxi at fifty feet. He transitioned to scan outside for the blinking light, while I stayed inside monitoring the instruments. We both flipped on our spotlights. When mine lit up the water below, I glanced, just for a second, down through the chin bubble.

Something about the way the chop was moving didn't compute in my brain. The waves appeared to be moving forward, away from us, rather than behind us, which would have made more sense with the wind direction and my assumed forward motion. This gave me the sense that I was backing down. In the fraction of a moment that it took me to process this information, stories crept into my consciousness of aircraft that had, in night overwater hovering profiles, inadvertently started backing down without the pilots recognizing it, and adjusting power to compensate for the loss of lift. In that moment, I immediately put my eyes back on the panel to get my scan back, but I knew I'd lost it, and I was tensing up, so my hands were delivering more exaggerated control inputs than normal—nothing dramatic, but I recognized that I needed some help to get back in the game.

The words that came out of my mouth were, "Get on the instruments." I waited a moment for a response from Bobby, trying to ingest the information in front of me, and deliver it to my hands and the plane, before I said it again, this time more forcefully. "Get on the instruments." He got the message the second time, and immediately said, "I have the controls." He transitioned to a forward climb, and we stabilized at 300 feet and cleaned up the aircraft for forward flight.

As we debriefed on what happened, I explained how I

CHAPTER 16: CONFESSIONS, STORIES & VOICES OF EXPERIENCE

thought I was backing down and had lost my scan. Bobby told me he thought I was talking to myself the first time I said to get on the instruments, but the second time he could tell from my voice that I was talking to him. He'd done exactly what he should do, which was to take the controls, and get us away from the water before asking questions. He'd had a good enough look around that flashing light to determine there wasn't a human attached to it, so we decided to call it a night, and head home. It took me fifteen minutes of straight-and-level flight, looking at the solid horizon of the Miami night skyline in front of us, to re-cage my internal gyro and get my head straight.

This whole episode was a non-event, really, because we relied on our training and crew resource management to prevent a bad situation from getting worse. But it shook my confidence. That it took me so long to re-cage after just a moment of spatial disorientation was a lesson that reinforced the mantra I'd heard hundreds of times before—when they're your primary source of accurate information about what the aircraft is doing, "stay on the instruments". After a few practice approaches to the water, I was back on my game, having learned a cheap lesson that stayed with me.

—**Commander Elizabeth Booker,** U.S. Coast Guard (Ret) H65 Dolphin helicopter pilot. https://aviatrixbookreview.com/

Next, we have a gripping tale from former Navy pilot Jim Tritten. Jim's story, lightly edited here, illustrates what's likely the most common break in the safety error chain, "Get home-itis." Here's Jim's story:

The evening of Sunday, December 22nd, 1968, I flew a single-engine propeller-driven aircraft, an A-1E Skyraider from Norfolk Virginia back to home base at Quonset Point, Rhode Island. Two young sailors were going to New England so I told them to get in…I would save them a bus fare.

I'd had my wings for about a year and a half, and I had nearly 750 hours in my logbook — not too bad for a twenty-three-year-old. I planned a longer, 600-mile, overland route because we hadn't worn our…exposure suits, which were required if we took a direct path over the frigid Atlantic Ocean. Since most of the east coast was just above freezing and socked in, I filed an instrument flight plan because our journey would be in the clouds until we flew east of the front. I would not be able to maintain visual contact with the ground or see the stars. No problem — I should have radio contact with helpful air traffic controllers and access to ground radio beacons along the way. I also wanted to get back home to Rhode Island — to my new wife, for the holidays.

CHAPTER 16: CONFESSIONS, STORIES & VOICES OF EXPERIENCE

As I pushed the throttle forward to takeoff power... The big radial engine shook the aircraft as we rolled forward. I pulled back on the stick, the 20,000 pounds of airplane eased off the tarmac and we climbed. I raised the landing gear and flaps — everything snug as I throttled back to normal climb power...we were swallowed by the dark gray clouds, and the foreboding night.

The cockpit was lit only by the dim red lights on the instrument panel. My crewman sat on the right — but he wasn't a pilot or a navigator... he couldn't help with any of the inflight duties... I switched a red lever over to take fuel from the external auxiliary tanks.

ATC informed me the weather along the northerly route towards New York City was deteriorating rapidly, with freezing rain and snow coming from the west. They advised me to fly...directly home to Rhode Island over the Atlantic and stay ahead of the front. Seems like the storm took a turn for the worse since I talked to the weather guessers a few minutes ago in Norfolk. As none of us wore exposure suits...I told the controllers I had to remain over land.

West of Newark, (NJ) my primary navigation receiver died...I couldn't get this backup system to point to any navigation station needed for my flight. I advised ATC that I had no operable onboard navigation systems. No big deal

I thought. I could still occasionally see the ground, and I could always navigate by following highways and cities under a visual flight rules plan.

A friendly voice advised me that they had me on their ground radar...(Then) the canopy clouded over, the Plexiglas sheathed in ice.

ATC advised there was freezing rain above me and again suggested I fly east over the Atlantic. I told the controller I needed a lower altitude to get to warmer temperatures and reiterated I couldn't fly over the ocean.

Since I wasn't getting any help from either my navigation aids or air traffic control...I canceled my instrument flight plan and told the controllers I was proceeding visually. The rotating green and white lights of a small civilian airport were ahead. I circled it while the wings thawed and tried to figure out what to do next. Land while I could see a runway? Or press on to Rhode Island and home?

Then the clear "sucker" hole I was in ended, and I was back in the opaque soup without an instrument flight plan or the ability to see the ground.

Shit.

We were flying over New York or New Jersey shopping centers...car headlights in parking lots. People likely

CHAPTER 16: CONFESSIONS, STORIES & VOICES OF EXPERIENCE

shopping for Christmas — I was no more than 500 feet above them. I wondered how low I could go and still keep above the hills and power lines.

I shot my hand forward, added full power, pulled back on the stick, and struggled to gain altitude — regardless of the ice above. I heard the comforting rumble of the powerful reciprocating engine with its sixteen-foot propeller washing the swirling wet sky over my wings and fuselage.

Without warning, the reassuring roar...was replaced by deafening silence! The sharp whistle of cold air screamed past the canopy as the plane plummeted on a descending glide slope through the clouds towards terra firma.

The engine had stopped!

My training kicked in again — the lack of sound caused my body to act without conscious thought. Looking to my right, the red fuel selection handle was pointed at the auxiliary tank. I had run the external fuel tank dry. I needed to manually switch to the full internal main tanks ...

The engine caught, and I slowly added power until we were able to climb away from a potential fiery grave—less than twenty seconds away, had I not acted. I checked my compass and pushed the stick and rudder until I again headed east. Moments later we broke out in the clear and the stars and the lights of New York's Westchester County lay ahead. All I needed to do was to fly southeast by the compass until I hit Interstate 95, then follow the road and the Connecticut shoreline east to Rhode Island to put an end to this ordeal.

I motored along the south shore of Connecticut, the dark of Long Island Sound on my right and the steady stream of white headlights on my left. I finished an uneventful remainder of the flight home and made a perfectly smooth, three-point landing.

That dark night, I knelt and kissed the asphalt tarmac of NAS Quonset Point, Rhode Island as the briny sea breeze from Narragansett Bay heralded the storms headed our way from the west. My knees were not quite steady on my way into the squadron's hangar. Mercifully, my crewman and the two passengers appeared blissfully unaware of how close they had come to being a part of some twisted flaming wreckage on a nameless patch of dirt. Instead, we all enjoyed a very Merry Christmas.

—Jim Tritten Commander U.S. Navy (ret)

Many pilots have been in Jim's cockpit. Needless to say, what drove Tritten's decisions were his focus on getting back to home base, completing the mission, saving his two passengers'

CHAPTER 16: CONFESSIONS, STORIES & VOICES OF EXPERIENCE

bus fare, and being home with a new spouse, always a strong incentive for a twenty-three-year-old. The error chain is pretty obvious here as well: Disregarding potentially perilous weather; leaving important equipment behind, and the limitations that entailed; over-reliance on single systems like navaids; and trying to stay visual rather than risk icing up the wings. But the biggest driver of the error chain in Jim's story is simple "Get-home-it is". Thanks, Jim Tritten for sharing this.

Next up, a tale from colleague Capt. Bill Collier USMCR and his initiation to flying with Air America in Laos:

> It was my second day of routine upcountry training in Laos with Air America. Until then, I'd only done routine touch-and-go landings around the Udorn, Thailand, airport, and local flight checks to see if I knew how to fly the H-34. Of course, I did. I'd recently flown 750 hours of serious combat in the machine in Vietnam. I was already feeling that I had more combat experience than the Air America instructors.
>
> Harry was showing me the ropes. We were flying routine resupply missions to local troops in a safe area about forty miles north of Vientiane. Harry did most of the flying, as he explained company operating procedures and rules and familiarized me with the area.
>
> We flew to one of the most challenging landing zones, a deep

cookie-cutter hole surrounded by 150-foot tall teak trees. A pilot doing one of those landings needed more than a little experience to land at the bottom of the hole without going splat. Harry carefully descended, and expertly landed the helicopter in the LZ. After a few local troops boarded, he said those magic words every pilot loves to hear, "You got it."

I took the controls and climbed straight up until we were hovering at 150 feet, looking out at a sea of treetops. At this point, it became obvious to both of us that we were too heavy. The proper procedure then would have been for me to hover carefully back down, land, and off-load a passenger or two.

Not me. My budding disdain for those Air America instructors allowed my Marine Corps pride, and my youthful arrogance, to override my common sense. I'll show this older former-Army fart how we Marines did it in Vietnam, I thought. I'd do a max-adrenaline "pump and dump" take off.

A pump and dump takeoff was something I'd done several times in Vietnam under fire. I pumped the collective lever up to give myself a momentary rise in elevation. I knew for certain that doing so would cause me to lose RPM, but I knew also I'd soon have ground effect to rely on, which would help me slide into translational lift. I was wrong. Very wrong!

CHAPTER 16: CONFESSIONS, STORIES & VOICES OF EXPERIENCE

The soft, leafy treetops were not a hard enough surface to provide ground effect, and I had no clear air under me to dive into in order to gain airspeed. I could NOT gain translational lift. We began to sink down into the sea of 150-foot tall teak trees. I had a fleeting vision of rotor blades hitting trees, bending, chopping off the tail; ruptured fuel cells ignited by broken wires … the perfect recipe for fire and explosion.

HOLY SHIT, we're going to die!

I fought to avoid the fiery crash. As we plummeted into the trees, the rotor blades chopped foliage around us. Bits of branches and leaves engulfed us, creating a green whirlpool swallowing us, blocking off all visibility. The more foliage we chopped, the more RPM we lost. The more RPM we lost, the faster we were sucked into the green vortex. There was no place to go but down into fiery oblivion. To the front and right side, visibility dropped to zero.

To the left, I spotted an area where the trees looked smaller and softer. I added all the power I could, pulling in full collective pitch to cushion our inevitable crash. To hell with the RPM and power limitations. If I could only get there, we might crash only once instead of two or three times as we flailed down through the trees.

I can't say that we landed. We simply ceased descending onto a small knoll covered by high elephant grass, reaching higher than the rotor blades, that is, until I unceremoniously mowed the grass off to rotor blade height. We were on the ground, intact, and not crispy fried to death in a steaming heap of burning rubble.

The green whirlwind continued swirling around us. The helicopter windows were obstructed by a thick, downy coating of freshly chopped vegetable fiber. As the debris settled out of the air, I saw pieces of brush and limbs all over the LZ. One small tree, almost three inches in diameter, was so close to the cockpit window I reached out and touched it. It was chopped off at rotor height.

Shit! Double SHIT! But we were still alive.

We had no choice but to shut down and assess the situation, and the damage to the aircraft. Miracles do happen. I'd barely avoided puncturing the belly of the aircraft (fuel tanks!) on a tree stump. The only damage to the helicopter was that three of the four rotor expendable blade tips were damaged. I'd intentionally ruined a number of them while flying in Vietnam, mowing my way through tall elephant grass into hillside LZs to rescue wounded Marines. Luckily, the tail rotor had no damage.

CHAPTER 16: CONFESSIONS, STORIES & VOICES OF EXPERIENCE

It took a while to hack away the brush and trees enveloping the helicopter, and to clean the greenish, fibrous coating off the windows.

I was surprised that Harry didn't simply return to base and say I was unfit to fly for the Company. I think the Company needed pilots badly. Had we crashed and survived, I'm sure I would have been fired.

At least I showed I had some balls. I didn't whimper or beg to apologize to Harry, as I probably should have for nearly killing us. I had had so many close calls in Vietnam that this little event really didn't faze me. But I did learn that I had to clean up my act and not do any more "Nam heroics" or I'd be soon unemployed. Or dead.

—Capt. Bill Collier USMCR, Vietnam, Laos, & Air America

Once you become a pilot you can find yourself in these cockpits as well. It's a sickening feeling to run out of altitude, ideas, airspeed, and rpm all at once. Both Jim Tritten's tale and Captain Bill's show that military pilots must let go of the "watch this shit" impulse once they're back in the real aviation world.

Next, a harrowing tale of ignored better judgment, unsecured cargo, a lost mailbag, followed by a trek through the enemy-infested jungle of Vietnam to retrieve it. This story is from a unit buddy from my tour in Vietnam. It gives an inside look at some of the hidden perils we faced in South Asia. Here, lightly edited, is David Trujillo's story:

> In November 1970, I was a Huey Aircraft Commander flying an "ash and trash mission" when a loadmaster asked if I could take a passenger. A captain wanted to fly (and) take pictures, since he'd never been out in the bush. I shouldn't have agreed to take him, because the aircraft was already overloaded, but I did.
>
> We headed toward our coordinates, west of the tallest peak in the area called Nui Kae, a mountain rising thousands of feet out of the jungle. We were about 1000 meters west of the summit, when the captain leaned out to take pictures. Suddenly, both my crewmembers swore out loud, and I feared that the captain had fallen out! But it wasn't that. The crew chief yelled, "Sir the captain just sent the mail bag out!"
>
> At least it wasn't another dead American, but the red mailbag was almost as important, with precious letters from home, care packages, pictures, Dear John letters, etc. I banked left, spun the helicopter into a 360-degree descent, and spotted the mailbag falling into the jungle. It came to rest in an area more or less devoid of jungle greenery (because of agent orange deforestation) and landed on a tree. There was no place to land close to the bag, so I

climbed back up and continued the mission, marking the location on my map.

Afterwards, I landed at the command firebase, shut down, and accompanied the captain to headquarters. Luckily, he told the commander the lost mailbag was his fault, and after I gave him the bag's coordinates, I was released to continue my missions.

Days later I got a call to come to our Battalion headquarters. The commander from the firebase and our Division XO were there. They'd postponed the captain's journey home and sent him out in charge of a platoon of troops to recover the mailbag, using my coordinates. But they were unable to find it, so the commanders were very upset. The mail was a morale booster for troops in the field. They asked me where I thought the bag was. I knew my coordinates were pretty good, so I proposed that they provide me a scout helicopter and I'd fly out to Nui Kae and get the bag for them. What was I thinking? Could my life be worth less than a mailbag?

The next day, the scout helicopter landed, and I got in with a borrowed M-16, my flight helmet, my survival vest with a PRC-90 radio, and my 38. pistol. We flew to Nui Kae, and in fifteen minutes I spotted the mailbag in a tree, six feet above the ground. The scout pilot couldn't land near it, but from a hover I could jump out and get the bag, 500 feet away. He wasn't keen on hovering there for twenty minutes, since it was enemy territory, so we agreed that he'd take off, fly around until I returned with the bag, and then I'd crawl back into his helicopter.

Well, the jungle looked pretty different on the ground than it did from the air, and as soon as he took off, I started toward what I thought was the mailbag tree. There were downed trees, rocks, bushes, tall grass in my way. I looked at my watch. It was taking too long for me to get to where the mailbag was. After a harrowing forty-minute scramble, I found the tree. Just then I heard the helicopter fly close by, then go to the uphill side of where I was. I thought, "what if he can't find me?" and it sent chills up my back. I wrestled with the tree, retrieved the bag, and started back to the touchdown place. Every sound I made I was aware of the threat of Viet Cong or NVA. I heard the scout helicopter pass about two football fields downhill from me. He was having trouble finding me, plus I knew he must be short on fuel.

Arriving at the touchdown zone, I hugged the ground and waited for the helicopter. It passed again, this time even further away from me! I turned on the radio and tried to contact him, but he was on the other side of the mountain.

CHAPTER 16: CONFESSIONS, STORIES & VOICES OF EXPERIENCE

The jungle was silent, except for mosquitos buzzing around. Straining to hear the chopper, instead I heard sounds of thrashing. An enemy patrol? I cocked my M-16. Something rustled in the bushes just eighty feet away!

Finally, the scout pilot answered. "Having trouble finding you, do you have a smoke grenade?"

I didn't, but I reached in my survival vest and took out a pin flare. "I have pin flares," I told him. I shot the flare, followed immediately by another one. Then I fired several rounds from the M-16 in the direction of the noise.

The scout pilot heard the M-16 fire and saw the pin flares. "Gotcha in sight" he said, and he circled around, appearing again just above me. He hovered to where I could lift the bag into the back of the aircraft, and then I crawled into the front seat.

The pilot took off, and we were both relieved and safe. I returned the mailbag to the firebase and was flown back to the Hideout (Home unit). No one ever thanked us for finding the bag. I'm grateful for the scout pilot, but I never got his name.

—David Trujillo Comanchero 32, Vietnam 1970-71 UH-1H

The lesson? Always secure cargo, pay attention to your weight and balance, even if you must refuse passengers, especially for photo ops. This story could have had a much different and very tragic ending. For one, Mr. Trujillo could have been killed or captured by "the bad guys," number two, the unsecured mailbag could have left the cargo bay and gone into the tail rotor of his Huey for a much different conclusion. Thanks, David, for sharing this lesson.

Next, a Vietnam War story from my colleague Rich Magner, and his advice on three basic aviation issues: Visibility, trusting the gauges, and different scan techniques. Here's his advice:

> **Getting comfortable with lowering visibility:** One of my first memories of flight school was a lesson I got from an old Navy WWII & Korean War vet, Wally Miracle. On a number of occasions, when the ceiling was low, Wally had me bump up into the clouds, then gradually descend for better visibility. It was a technique probably frowned upon now, but it made me comfortable with clouds. I learned not to panic and to make gradual corrections. From crew comments, (years later) I think I flew higher than many of the other pilots, especially at night, as I felt it gave me a better indication of lowering visibility & ceiling, adding to my situational awareness.
>
> **On trusting the gauges:** In Vietnam one 0'dark-thirty

night, I was flying south towards Dau Tieng for Quan Loi. It was very dark, with a high ceiling, and just two or three visible ground lights. I began having an eerie discomfort I'd never experienced before. I asked the other pilot to take the controls, and in less than a minute, I snapped out of it and was back to normal. That's when I began using a different scan for nights versus days. There have been numerous times over the years when I've experienced that eerie feeling, reminding me to bring my scan inside the cockpit more.

On instrument scan: I always enjoyed night flying, in spite of the downside of being tired. I found a few pilots who were uncomfortable with flying at night. A common trait was that their night scan didn't differ from their day scan. As an instructor, I had them reverse their daytime exterior & interior scan percentages and that seemed to help.

—**Rich Magner is a retired commercial helicopter pilot, and a Vietnam veteran.**

Bob Weil's story reminds us of a few perils unique to aviation, especially long-duration missions. This couldn't happen today with modern navaids like GPS etc. But even today, aircrafts don't have low-tech items like alarm clocks! Here's commander Weil's story:

In the 1970's, I was flying C-141A's for the US Air Force out of Norton AFB, California. Most of our missions were in support of the war in Vietnam and I flew one to two trips a month, usually, in that direction. Our duty days were generally long (sixteen hours) with very little downtime for the two to three weeks we were gone, so max jet lag.

South Vietnam had fallen in 1975, but we were still flying over it on the way to Thailand. On one flight after that, my aircraft was MEACONED (false VOR signal) off course over Vietnam, over a probable SAM (Surface-to-Air Missile) site.

After that incident, we had to fly around South Vietnam by flying to their airspace, turning left to parallel it, then turn right going due west until another right turn took us north to Thailand over the South China Sea. All this with no GPS or "modern" navigation aids. Just a navigator with a sextant, a doppler, and a watch.

So, there I was, (I love stories that start that way), flying along at FL350 in a C-141A in early 1976. I had a crew of seven, and we had departed Clark AFB in the Philippines before sunrise. As we neared the Saigon FIR (Flight Information Region), we were anticipating the turn southbound and away from the home of the SAM's. We were more relaxed as we turned west.

CHAPTER 16: CONFESSIONS, STORIES & VOICES OF EXPERIENCE

This is where I fell asleep. I'm not sure how long I was out, but when I woke up I looked around the cockpit and everyone else was asleep, too. I stretched and looked down. WE WERE OVER LAND! The whole trip around Vietnam was (supposed to be) over water! I checked the autopilot, and we were still at FL350 and heading west, but what country were we over? I woke the crew, but the navigator didn't know where we were either. I wish I'd paid more attention in Geography class! What country is southwest of Vietnam at the end of a westbound leg in the South China Sea? According to the current time we should have turned north earlier, so I turned north-northeast to intercept our planned course. At least radar wasn't common in Southeast Asia at that time, and position reports were the only way to keep track of traffic. I tuned in the Bangkok VOR, but it was still too far away.

Speeding up to make up for the extra time we had taken, I gave position reports of where we were supposed to be. Finally, we received the Bangkok VOR and got on the flight-planned course, landing only a few minutes later than anticipated. I love it when you can make the plan come together anyway!

It wasn't until a week or so later, when I got home, that I was able to look on a world map to see where we had been.

Malaysia, as it turned out. Lessons learned: 1. The pilots can't all sleep at the same time in flight; 2. Study world maps for the area you're flying in; 3. Kiss your GPS every day!

—**Robert Weil** is a retired aviator with active service in the US Air Force where he flew C-141s. Weil flew for Continental Airlines for five years. His Army service includes thirteen years as a full-time instructor with the Iowa National Guard where he flew the UH-1, and CH-47 Chinook. Bob and his wife Cindy live in Florida.

Next, we have a tale from a colleague in the Ohio National Guard, and a former UH-1 pilot. This story shows why situational awareness is so important, even before you enter the cockpit.

I was doing a night Additional Flight Training Period (AFTP) with one of the senior Warrant officers in a Huey (UH-1). We went up to Bluffton (Ohio) to eat at the little restaurant there beside the airport. The tarmac area was pretty cluttered with fixed-wing aircraft, so we landed in the grassy area beside one of the hangars.

It was already dark when we landed and the bottom had fallen out of the thermometer after a sunny, warm (upper thirties) day. When we came out of the restaurant it had hit the low twenties. Have an idea where this story is going?

CHAPTER 16: CONFESSIONS, STORIES & VOICES OF EXPERIENCE

I was on the controls, and I fired up the aircraft (wasn't starting a Huey the greatest sound in the world?) I started to get light...the right skid broke free, but the left remained frozen...stupid instinct...snap cyclic right, and jerk collective.

Fortunately, I had a guardian angel putting pressure on the collective. I felt pressure on the pedals, and (the aircraft) yawed just enough to break free. Nevertheless, we had been well on our way into dynamic rollover, and probably a class A accident. It was a pretty quiet flight home as I recall.

—Maj. Steve Kline (Ret) OHARNG

What Steve describes is a common scenario. The landing gear of his helicopter was iced to the ground on the left side. When he added power, the skid that was free, the right-side gear lifted, but the left one didn't. Our instinct in a helicopter is to think more power is always the best way out of trouble. This is clearly not the case. (The "class A" he mentions is the aircraft accident category, class A being the highest, with an aircraft destroyed).

Thanks to all my contributors to this section, it's potentially embarrassing to admit our aviation close calls and mishaps. But one thing we learn pretty early in our flying career is that there are no new ways to crash and bust up an aircraft. They've all been done at one time or another.

We learn from others' mistakes, miscues, oversights, and errors. There's no reason to do them over. Here's a suggestion for a foggy, no-fly afternoon: Pull up a few NTSB accident reports, read them over, put yourself in those cockpits, keep an open mind, and you'll learn something. Remember that those chronicles of cockpit carelessness and confusion that led to accidents could happen to you. Don't judge those pilots. It could be *your* name in that report. Learn from them and you'll be a better aviator.

Chapter 17

YOU CAN FLY

Yes, You Can Fly!

Our first "Yes you can" story is from Mandy Hickson, a self-described "fast-jet pilot" with the Royal Air Force, (RAF) and only the second woman to fly the GR-4 Tornado in combat. Ms. Hickson's story is about a young woman who thought she couldn't fly—until Hickson took her flying. Here is "Flying with Emily":

> Having served as a fast jet pilot in the Royal Air Force (RAF) for seventeen years, I decided it was time to leave for pastures new, but I wasn't quite ready to let go completely, so I joined the Air Experienced Flight at Ministry of Defense (MOD) Boscombe Down, UK as a Volunteer Reservist. I then flew the Tutor aircraft and took air cadets, aged between thirteen and eighteen, on a flying experience that they would hopefully never forget.
>
> It was on a full flying day that I had the pleasure of flying with a young girl called Emily. We flew four cadets in the morning, and four in the afternoon and, as you can imagine, by the eighth trip of the day you were feeling slightly less inspiring and motivated than you were on the first. That was when I saw Emily for the first time. She was walking out to the aircraft with her shoulders stooped, and a slightly surly look on her face. I introduced myself and told her what I had planned for the next exciting thirty

CHAPTER 17: YOU CAN FLY

minute flying experience. I was met with a series of grunts that I could only translate as teenager-speak for "how wonderful - that sounds like great fun"! It transpired that this was Emily's first flight in any aircraft and when I asked her if she was excited, I was simply met by a monosyllabic reply!

We took to the skies. It was a beautiful day with a pure blue sky interspersed with a few white fluffy clouds, the sort of day that is a pilot's dream. I started off by demonstrating the basic controls, left, right, up and down..."you have control Emily" I said. "Hmph hmph hmph, ma'am!" I heard in response. Emily seemed strangely relaxed though, and she flew the aircraft really well. I decided to challenge her a little more. I demonstrated how to turn the aircraft, first simple, thirty-degree angle of bank turns. These provided no problem to her, so I threw down the gauntlet with sixty-degree turns. Now these are more challenging to any pilot because, if you don't raise the nose and add power, you start a rather ominous spiral descent. Unperturbed, Emily maneuvered the aircraft as if she had been behind the controls all her life.

With the cotton wool clouds calling we decided to have a little fun, diving through gaps and gullies in the clouds as if we were taking on an undiscovered landscape, designed by the Gods. Great fun that even the surliest of teenagers could not help but enjoy.... But still not even a smile from my silent co-pilot!

The finale came in the form of aerobatics—ballet dancing in the skies. Once again, I demonstrated how to perform a series of tumbles and turns, starting with a wonderful "loop the loop". Now if a loop is flown perfectly, as you pull out the bottom of the maneuver you will fly through the same piece of air that you disturbed on the way in, and the whole aircraft can shake quite violently. I always take the time to explain this, as it can come as a real shock to cadets when they experience it for the first time. I flew my loop very smoothly, but alas, at the bottom a smooth pullout, with no shaking. I handed the controls to Emily, following through on my own controls in case the maneuver didn't go according to plan, but there was no need as it was flown perfectly. As she pulled out of the bottom, the whole aircraft started shaking as we flew through the previously disturbed air. Emily turned to look at me with a huge smile on her face. I translated this look as "I am better than you!" I upped the pace, challenging her with more and more complex aerobatics and they were all flown in the same confident manner.

After returning to the base, I turned to Emily and said, "I

CHAPTER 17: YOU CAN FLY

know you have spent the last thirty minutes grunting at me, I'm not even sure that you've enjoyed it, but can I just say that in twenty years of flying, I've never flown with anyone who has demonstrated as much natural ability as you have just done".

"I bet you say that to everyone," she retorted gruffly.

"I've not actually, I've never said it to anyone. Is this something that you may want to do in the future-to pursue a career as a pilot?"

It was at that moment that Emily looked straight at me, making eye contact for the first time. Her entire body language changed, her defenses fell away, and she said, "Yes, it is, actually. This is something I've always wanted to do, but I never thought I'd be good enough. I've dreamed about being a pilot all my life, and I thought, what happens if I came along today and I was rubbish at it? I thought it was better not to try, then if I failed, I would be able to blame it on the fact that I hadn't tried".

I've thought about this so often since, and it always makes me think. How often do you steer away from taking on a new challenge or experience because you're worried you might fail? I'm sure we're all guilty of this at some point in our lives, but until you try you never know what you are good at. Once you have a goal to visualize, it's always easier to work towards it, to focus on it. So whatever your ambition is.....Dream it, Believe it, Do it!

-(Mandy Hickson, "Dream it, Believe it, Do it" in *An Officer, Not a Gentleman* ©2020, used with permission.)

—**Mandy Hickson** was only the second woman to fly a Tornado GR4 on the front line. She completed three tours of duty, and forty-five missions over Iraq. Mandy Hickson is the author of *An Officer, Not a Gentleman* and motivational speaker at Hickson Ltd., https://hicksonltd.com/

MayCay Beeler refers to herself as an aviatrix, authorpreneur, adventurer, motivator, and mom. We're not sure which role is more dangerous, but here are a few clues. Let the reader decide.

As a TV Personality, I initially learned to fly for a television assignment that would charm, craft, and change the course of my life in unexpected ways. Through my passionate ongoing work as a professional pilot, aviation author, journalist, speaker, and founder of my signature flight program, "The Diva Flight Experience", I share the joy of flight with others by affirming what I know for sure: Life is full of possibilities. Never tell people your dreams; Show

CHAPTER 17: YOU CAN FLY

them. It's all connected—your gifts, your circumstances, your purpose, your imperfections, your journey, your destiny. Embrace them. The privilege of a lifetime is being who you are.

As a young girl, I wanted to grow-up to be an astronaut, but my eyesight was not perfect (a strict requirement at the time). I also lacked confidence, wondering if I was even smart enough to consider such a lofty profession. As fate would have it, I would grow up to be a world record-breaking pilot, and award-winning Flight Instructor, so apparently, I was more capable than I knew.

When a desire/goal/dream speaks to your heart, it's important to listen. Give it a shot. Believe in yourself. If you fail, you fail, but you may succeed. You never know unless you try. We've all heard the stories of famous people who failed dozens of times before finally succeeding at their goals. There's nothing wrong with failing. It's part of the process. But there's great sadness in not trying.

Never fear what your peers may say if you fall short. There will be critics. They may gossip, but will forget about you soon enough, as they move on to the next target to criticize. What they think doesn't matter. What you think about yourself does.

My advice for young folks seeking a pilot career is to find a quality flight instructor you feel good about. One who cares about you. If you struggle, and this is normal in certain phases of flight training, your CFI should be able to nurture and encourage you, finding ways that help you as an individual achieve your personal best. Don't compare yourself to others with similar goals. It's never about them. It's about you. This is your life journey. We all learn differently at our own pace, and in our own way. You need a CFI who understands this so she/he can best guide you to master the material and maneuvers. It can be difficult at times, especially if you reach Airline Transport Pilot (ATP) Certificate status. You have to really want it.

As a Flight Instructor, I've had the privilege of helping countless students earn their wings. It's a rewarding honor to see them achieve this dream. A few have suffered through the process because they didn't truly want it. They were learning to fly only to please or impress others. I recall two different female pilots who tolerated their training, never enjoying it, because their professional Airline Pilot Dads and Granddads expected them to follow in their footsteps. One of those women made it to the airline (using) her pilot family connections ensuring that she was hired, yet her heart wasn't in it. I was saddened that she suffered through it all just to please others.

CHAPTER 17: YOU CAN FLY

Make sure whatever goal you pursue, you do it for you. Life is too short to live someone else's dream. Being true to yourself is key.

We know women can reach new heights in an arena traditionally known as a boys' club. I founded "The Diva Flight Experience" to empower gals with the thrill of personally piloting an aircraft. See www.divaflight.com.

My life story is about making the most of every moment; stepping up to the plate; making my life count and encouraging others to do the same.

—**MayCay Beeler** is a record-breaking pilot, former TV personality, best-selling, award-winning author, Airline Transport Pilot, *FAA Certificated Flight Instructor and Founder of The Diva Flight Experience.* www.maycaybeeler.com

Next, we have another voice from the cockpit, a wonderful story of one woman's realization that, even though "good girls do not fly," as she was told, Capt. Judy Rice was not about to let that bogus admonition stand in her way. Here's Capt. Rice's story:

"You are a girl. Good girls do not fly." I dreamt of flying as long as I can remember. After hearing these devastating words, I kept my dream a secret. I was a "good girl", and I did not want to disappoint anyone.

As a toddler, my dream momentarily surfaced. I recall vividly one evening hearing a loud WOOSH! WOOSH!! I ran outside, amazed at what was overhead. I couldn't speak, just stared at the large hot air balloon gliding over my house. The balloonist hollered down, "What's a matter little girl, cat got your tongue?!"

It took forty plus years to gain the courage for a discovery flight. This was the beginning for discovering myself. When solo approached, I was terrified and unsure I could safely command the airplane. After all, "good girls do not fly." Through this experience, I gained self-confidence, and for the first time, had command of my destiny.

I strongly encourage you to further recognize yourself in reading *PostFlight: An Old Pilot's Logbook* by Byron Edgington. It's never too early or too late to begin taking command of your life.

—**Capt. Judy Rice**, Think Global Flight Earthrounder, world speed record, certificated flight instructor, and author. www.captainjudy.com, www.thinkglobalflight.org

You're never too young to start. Just ask FO Courtney Robson. Courtney provided her story of discovering aviation, and "being hooked" as she says, acquiring her private certificate at seventeen. She's now just twenty-three years old and flying for PSA airlines. Here's Courtney's story:

CHAPTER 17: YOU CAN FLY

My father is the foundation of my love for flying. He's a pilot at Delta Air Lines and encouraged me to pursue aviation from a young age. In 2013, I had the privilege to take a Young Eagles flight with EAA member Richard White at Triangle North Executive Airport (LHZ). After that day, my father signed me up for flying lessons at Wings of Carolina Flying Club in Sanford, NC (TTA). I finished my Private Pilot Certificate when I was seventeen and was hooked! While studying Economics at North Carolina State University I completed my Commercial, CFI, and CFII. During my last year of college, FlightGest Academy hired me to teach at Raleigh-Durham airport, (RDU) and I fell in love with introducing new people to aviation. Watching my students grow in their flying skills made teaching very rewarding, and I still keep in touch with them.

At Causey Aviation, a 135 operation, I built more flight experience, and their Director of Operations (DO) hired me to fly their Citation V. Upon reaching 1,500 hours, I was hired by PSA Airlines as a First Officer on their Canadair Regional Jets. Now at twenty-three years old, you will find me flying out of the Charlotte Douglas International Airport (CLT) working flights throughout the Midwest and Eastern United States. My goal is to be a widebody captain flying all over the world.

The Ninety-Nines, Professional Pilot Leadership Initiative, Women in Aviation, Civil Air Patrol, and the EAA are organizations that have helped me progress to where I am today, and I am so grateful for the people I have met and worked with. Lessons I've learned are to be grateful, humble, and learn something new every day.

—**Courtney Robson** is a First Officer at PSA Airlines based in Charlotte, NC.

Thank you, Courtney, and all those who contributed to this chapter. Aviation is a collaborative endeavor, and more so when advice is being dispensed.

Now we hear from Colleen Nevius, a Naval Aviator, and retired Captain who flew helicopters for the US Navy.

Growing up the eldest of six into a Naval Aviation family, I was a mystery to my mother. She'd been a model and a girly girl, but bless her, she encouraged me to be who I was!

Dad, a Navy pilot, encouraged me to do whatever I put my mind to. His advice? Be in the right place at the right time with the right tools and you'll be there to sprint in when the door cracks open. Prophetic.

During my junior year of high school, the Navy opened flight training to women. They'd go on to jobs in the

CHAPTER 17: YOU CAN FLY

squadrons that performed non-combat functions: target towing, hurricane hunting, executive transport, electronic warfare, and shore-based utility work. When I saw an article in Parade magazine about these women, I saw it as a sign…my father had been right. The doors were ajar, and I was going to get there as the world of Naval Aviation grew to find a place for women pilots. The next year, a limited number of women were accepted into the Navy Reserve Officer Training Corp (NROTC), and my path was clear… this was my opportunity to fly. Something I'd never done before…hmm.

In August 1973 I joined the NROTC at Purdue University. My grades and participation earned me a full scholarship, and I pursued a Bachelor of Science hoping it would improve my chances for flight school selection. Summer NROTC training that year included flight time in a small aerobatic airplane, and then a helicopter. As I got into the front seat of the helo, the pilot picked up to a low hover, backed out of the parking spot, and zoomed out over Padre Island Sound. THIS WAS FLYING!

In May 1977 I graduated from Purdue, and was commissioned in the Navy. Selected for pilot training, commencing October 1977, I flew the T-28, TH-57 and H-1, earning my coveted Wings of Gold in February

1979 in my first choice: helicopters. When I started flight training, women were barred from spending the night aboard navy ships. To my intense relief, the laws changed to allow women to serve temporarily aboard Navy ships, and I was one of the first two women pilots chosen for sea-duty flight assignment. I was sent to Helicopter Combat Support Squadron Six (HC-6) at NAS Norfolk, VA along with Lt. Karen Thornton, flying the H-46 Sea Knight performing Vertical Replenishment (VertRep) missions. Right time, right place, right toolbox.

In those early days, the Navy struggled to balance politics and PR against operational necessity, and politics initially prevailed. Lt. Thornton and I were assigned to shorter North Atlantic and Baltic NATO exercises, flying passengers and cargo rather than the expected six-month sea rotation aboard Mediterranean-bound supply ships.

In 1982, following my shipboard deployments, I was the first woman pilot selected to attend the Naval Test Pilot School, graduating in Class 83. Assigned to Rotary-Wing Aircraft Test Directorate as lead pilot for H-46 and CH-53E helicopters, I completed over 50 projects in a two-year assignment in the Attack Assault Branch, and was inducted as a member of the esteemed Society of Experimental Test Pilots.

CHAPTER 17: YOU CAN FLY

My next assignment took me to HM-12 Sea Component, and then HC-2, as Assistant Officer in Charge and Maintenance Officer, flying the CH-53E performing Vertical Onboard Delivery (VOD) missions. I led detachments of up to six pilots, fifty maintainers, and two aircraft deployed to NAS Roosevelt Roads, PR in support of carrier operations, and to Norway providing shore-based support for NATO exercises.

At no time do I recall anyone telling me that I couldn't. The vast majority of my bosses were very supportive…once I'd made my way. I followed a path of my own making, sometimes uncertain but always optimistic. I had incredible opportunities, and even better lifelong friends from a satisfying, 26-year Naval Aviation career.

—**Colleen Nevius** Capt. US Navy (ret.)

Thank you for that inspiring story, Capt. Nevius. It proves that those who have support can do anything they choose.

A note to young women reading this. First, thank you for taking the time. I know you'd rather be flying than reading about it. I'd rather be flying than *writing* about it! Here's a note of affirmation for you.

In our society women are routinely denied agency, and safety, and the privilege that piloting one's own life affords.

Aviation can give you those things, plus a level of freedom that's unavailable to other people, *especially* women. It allows you to move into the left seat of your own life, where any sensible adult wants and needs to be.

For that reason, it will be a sign of success for me if my book affirms even one young woman to achieve her dream to fly. When women make up only six percent of the pilot population, it's obvious to this old pilot that things need to change. We need to recognize that aircraft don't know about gender, or any other marker. Aircraft recognize, and respond, to competence.

I've always attempted to lift other people to a higher, more fulfilling level, especially women. Lifting people higher was, after all, my job description as a pilot, and I was very good at it. Writing is not my preferred activity to elevate others. I'd still rather be flying. But writing is a decent, and an honorable substitute. So that's one reason I wrote *Postflight: An Old Pilot's Logbook*.

Women gaining their agency is no small thing. Along with your freedom comes responsibility, of course. Aviation is a way for you to prove, if only to yourself, that you're competent, and important, and that you have dignity, and control over your life and destiny. Here's hoping you not only fly, but that you soar!

Chapter 18

Final Remarks

TIPS FROM YOUR CO-PILOTS

This part includes quotes I've received from aviation colleagues, your co-pilots.

If you have advice based on your own experience, I'd love to hear from you. And if you disagree with something you've found here, or if you have a better method, or a different and better perception of something, I'd like to hear that as well.

I try to take my own advice and remain humble about such things. The only reason I wrote the book in the first place was not out of a need to preach. Far from it. Finishing my career in 2005, after flying for fifty years, I don't just have a right to peddle advice; I have an obligation to do so. Once you've retired from the cockpit following a very long and satisfying career, you'll feel the same way.[24] Here's the summary:

Randy Mains:

Time spent on diagnosis is time well spent.

Consultation is not a sign of weakness—Use your resources.

No heroes! Consult other crewmembers, ATC, maintenance etc.

Decisions should always be reviewed.

Changing a decision is not indecision.

You have a right and responsibility as a professional to say, "No".

If someone says, "This is stupid", or if you power down twice in cruise flight, put the aircraft on the ground.

CHAPTER 18: FINAL REMARKS

—**Randy Mains** CRM instructor, contact info: info@Randymains.com

Ed Shoemaker: (Behind and getting behinder?) Land the damn helicopter!

Jake Molter: At the end of the day, any decision made for convenience is probably the wrong one. (See Get-Home-Itis)

Peter Murray: If there is doubt then there is no doubt! (Author: See CRM error chain, 'confusion')

Kevin C. Brandt: No matter how many hours or ratings you get, don't wear your hours on your sleeve, and always be a student. Remember, if you get 70% (on a test), they call you a pilot.

Keith Besherse: None of the (flying) tasks by themselves are all that hard. Anyone of average intelligence and hand-eye coordination can learn them.

Trygve Hestvik: Going to work as a pilot is like being a referee in the Super Bowl. If nobody talks about you at the end of the day, job well done!

—Trygve Hestvik went to Haugesund Maritime Tekniske Videregående Skole.

Mark Forsyth

There's no such thing as a fully trained pilot.

Always know where the wind is.

Don't assume anything.

It's good to trust; it's better to check.

Steven Clarke: It's better to be on the ground wishing you were in the air, than in the air wishing you were on the ground.

Mark Bonifache: Being a good pilot is about judgment, and judgment is two parts: experience and knowledge. When you first start out, knowledge is the crutch you'll lean on as you build experience. So, STUDY. When you have both experience and knowledge, you should have judgment and be flying and performing at a high level.

But be cautious as you grow older, be careful not to use your experience as a crutch and let your knowledge dwindle. Plenty of experienced pilots have paid the ultimate price for mistakes they should have known better than to make.

—Mark Bonifache is with Pinochet Helicopter Tours

CHAPTER 18: FINAL REMARKS

Jim Linehan: The day you come in to work and don't learn something, is the day you should hang up your wings.

Steve Hill: Speaking from experience, always wear clean underwear. Also, seek out a mentor with years of experience. Their knowledge and advice is priceless. Instructor pilots with 400 hours do not have institutional knowledge.

—**Steve Hill** Worked with U.S. Army, and he studied at Embry-Riddle Aeronautical University Worldwide

Capt. Bill Collier: Never let your exuberance—or arrogance—outfly your experience

—**Capt. Bill Collier** USMCR flew for the US Marine Corps in Vietnam, and for Air America in Laos.

Rich Burke: Plan your flight on the ground, execute the plan in flight. Kind of the Proper Prior Planning Prevents Piss Poor Performance theory. Nothing frustrated me more than someone trying to do it all on the fly, which often results in them being "behind the aircraft."

Kevin Warner: The more frequently you fly the cheaper your training will be. Longer periods between times = less retention.

James Todd Rolfe: ALWAYS have an out. (note all caps)

C.J. Chalue: Get an instructor that you click with. Don't be afraid to change instructors or flight schools if you feel you're being treated poorly. Flight schools are a business, and not everyone deserves or needs you.

Also, you need to read the supplements section of your aircraft manuals. Many pilots/students use the standard checklist from the manufacturer, but it specifically says it's not to be used like that. The supplements have additional information to be added to the preflight, startup etc. I usually make my own checklist for this reason.

It's OK to change schools and instructors. You're paying a lot of money, so you need to find a good fit. Also, once you find your fit, it's ok to change sometimes and fly with different instructors so you can get new insights if you're struggling with a specific topic or maneuver. In essence, take charge of your own education!

Kerry Stanley:

You don't know it all and you never will.

The checklist is your best friend.

Know your wind and weather.

Power lines kill. Always know where you're flying.

Pre planning your flight will save you.

Your mechanic is your best friend.

CHAPTER 18: FINAL REMARKS

Jim Henderson:

Rule No. 1 .... don't crash.

Rule No. 2 .... make sure the customer signs the flight report.

There ain't no other rules needed. Other than that, always wear what you'd walk home in.

Lee Rhodes: Establish your own personal weather limits and stick to them. That way...no more stomach cramps.

Terry Lay: Always keep a logbook and make a small note of what is entailed. It can help your past, present, and future. Now that I'm retired, (forty-four years/15,000 hrs) and seventy-two-years-old, sometimes family or friends ask when did you do, "this or that?" and I'll say, "I'll have to check my logbook." Then it brings back such good memories.

November Victor Charlie: (Keep) a handwritten logbook with room for notes. I know you can keep it online, or on your phone, and wherever else... but in thirty years you'll appreciate that you have a real logbook.

(An old pilot: I agree. One of my bigger regrets is that I didn't keep an actual logbook in Vietnam, dammit! How many times do I wish I had!)

Ray Trygstad: Always take a book so you have something to read if you have to make an emergency landing. I've landed in the backlot of a school, and in a garbage dump. When I was flying at sea, I kept a book in a waterproof pouch in my flight suit to read in the raft if the aircraft went in the water. I never did, and I never needed it! The corollary is to bring a deck of cards. Once you get set up in your survival situation, start playing solitaire, and in no time someone will (come) by to point out that the red eight needs to go on the black nine!

David Mabe: (In a request to me for inclusion in this book) Tell people how to study for and take the tests. Keys to success are a ticket to train, and every flight is a training flight.

—**David Mabe** is a Former Agent/ Pilot at CBP Air and Marine Operations.

Darren Kemp: Before spending your money on ground school, get the books and read the material. Do it to understand the concepts. Then let your CFI/II hone it in for you.

Tim Adamsen: Don't get a huge loan to pay for your instruction. Get a good job with benefits, then fly as much as you can on your off time in your own airplane. Sitting around a flight school hoping for flight hours for a full-time job will take forever. If you want to quit that good job, and fly for starvation wages, give it some thought. Aviation companies are notorious for going bankrupt, taking your retirement, and cutting your pay. Think twice about leaving a good, stable job to be a pilot. I bought into the "Pilot shortage" (story) in the '80s. It was all BS cooked up by FAPA. The airlines wanted military pilots.

So have multiple skillsets; you will need them. Flying for a living becomes work and not fun. Then you get laid off. If you are lucky enough to be hired by an airline that's in business long enough for you to retire, keep your retirement yourself. The Pension Benefit Guarantee fund is a poor living.

If you can get into the military as a pilot, do it. It's the best training…and you can stay in the Guard or Reserve till (age) sixty. Ex-military will be first in line for the best flying jobs

—Tim Adamsen, A&P Mechanic & project manager: Army Aviation Heritage Foundation.

John Mark Reid: Aviation is full of egos. Some of those egos will express negativity as an effort to bolster their own standing. When you encounter those people, move-on. Don't let anyone deter you from your goals.

Pete Laitinen: (Note: A whimsical bit of reverse psychology)

Never preflight your helicopter. Your risk of leaving an oil cap off, or a latch undone, is greater than your probability of finding something wrong. Just untie the rotor, check to see if there's a puddle underneath it, and hop in.

Never use a checklist. When Richie Rich charters your aircraft and sees you fumbling around with the instructions he'll think, "I'm never calling this guy again, he doesn't even know how to start the blooming thing." Just get in, buckle up, light it off, and pull pitch.

Never get a chart out in flight. If Richie Rich sees you looking at a map he's thinking, "Great, now this guy has gotten us lost out here in the middle of BFE." Just memorize frequencies, identifiers, and the general on-course headings, and pretend you know the area like the back of your hand.

Make sure you have your smokes in one pocket, your Ray Bans in the other, and get going.

(An old pilot: Pete, thanks for lightening things up just a bit! I can't find BF on my Egypt Sectional chart. It must be outdated!)

Bruce J. Scott: If you're forced to choose, your airplane may fly over gross weight, but it won't fly without fuel. (An old pilot: There's a story here, I suspect)

CHAPTER 18: FINAL REMARKS

Jason Kornder:

Have at least a passing familiarity of what (the mechanics) are talking about if they describe a repair. Even better, get them to show you. You will learn, and you'll make them happy. Also...

Ice is WAY heavier than it looks.

A forced IFR recovery isn't going to impress the client.

Make the weather call early and stick to it.

Learn your 'met' (weather). It's boring, but it will save your ass when the forecast is sketchy, and your knowledge is solid.

Cars work better than helos in bad weather. (The client sometimes needs to be reminded.)

Never stop learning. I learned way more from teaching and giving checkrides than I did during line jobs.

Be smart enough to understand that you don't know what you don't know.

Last, if you have to take a cab to your parking spot past all the empty ones, it's a sign. Ask someone what you did, and don't do it again.

(An old pilot: Sometimes as rookies we screw the pooch and don't even know it! Thanks, Jason Kornder.)

John Fraley: Aviation weather forecasts are half right half the time.

—**John Fraley** works at American Airlines.

Thomas Mann: Never be afraid to say, "No". Never be afraid to ask questions. Be as humble as you can be. Learn something new every day. Know your own limitations. Respect the aircraft. (See 'Dayno,' Chapter 15)

Len Klopper: Make very sure you know where the wind is coming from when you go for a pee behind the hangar!

—**Len Klopper** is owner of Cape Recreational flight training

Hayden Goldman: To climb the ladder of success in the (aviation) industry, be ready to be a gypsy. Be willing to migrate to the opportunities. Along the way, don't be an @hole. Networking and reputation are HUGE.

—**Hayden Goldman** is a R-W pilot at LA Water & Power

Dennis Hopping: Don't exceed your limitations or your helicopter's limitations whichever comes first. Of course, one has to be able to recognize their limitations first.

Don Jones: Never let a Bullfrog mouth overload your Tadpole ass.

CHAPTER 18: FINAL REMARKS

Micah Settle: Take the time to get to know your mechanics. Don't just complain about the problem and walk away. If they're braving the heat or cold weather to fix the issue, spending time to lend a helping hand can go a long way. Humility can speak volumes. Also, things that do you no good in aviation:

Runway behind you

Fuel back in the tank

Sky above you

Your mechanic's insight

Thirty seconds ago

—**Micah Settle** works at Air Life of Georgia

Steve Shailer: Don't make yourself famous.

—**Steve Shailer** is with Abu Dhabi Aviation

Christian D. Cattell: If assigned an altitude, be AT that altitude. Same with heading and airspeed. If you're supposed to do something, do it. If you're not supposed to, don't.

Laith Coory: Get into it with another trade to fall back on. Aviation is unpredictable.

Gunnar Martin: Don't love helicopters enough to get A.I.D.S…(especially) if you have kids. Fly less and parent more.

Wendy: Air Kauai, April 2005: "No rain; No rainbows!"

Colten Christopher Fronk: Some flight schools require it, but you need to…go help work on the aircraft. It helps build trust in your mechanics and to be more familiar with the helicopter, especially in emergencies.

Robert Black: Sometimes it's good to fly close to the flame, see and experience the heat, but then fly away again to survive, wiser in the art of heat.

Aviation truism: Takeoffs are optional; Landings are mandatory.

Aviation truism: The law of gravity is not a general rule.

Curtis Tyrone Jones: It's better to arrive late in this world than early in the next.

Joe Bradley: If you're just in it for the money and not the love of flying, you're in the wrong job.

John Glenn: I was sold on flying as soon as I had a taste for it.

CHAPTER 18: FINAL REMARKS

Antoine de Saint-Exupéry: I fly because it releases my mind from the tyranny of petty things.

Sarge *Whitley in Waiting for Willie Pete:* Education's important, but aviation's importanter!

LESSON ROUNDUP

Lessons Chapter 1

- Take opportunities to fly when and where you find them.
- Never doubt your own ability.
- Find a tough instructor.
- Show up ready to commit aviation.
- Timing is everything.

Lessons Chapter 2

- Becoming a pilot is worth it, but only if you believe it is.
- To solo in this hyper-protective world is almost too rewarding.
- A life in aviation isn't easy, predictable, romantic, or enriching, at least in terms of dollars, but you'll never regret it.
- Precision is the mark of an aviator. Strive for it.
- Remember, you're always a student.

Lessons Chapter 3

- Fly the aircraft with your head, not your hands and feet.

CHAPTER 18: FINAL REMARKS

- Ask questions, veteran pilots are always happy to help.
- Make sure you're medically qualified to fly.
- Flying isn't difficult, but it demands precision.
- A flying club can be a great resource.

Lessons Chapter 4

- Fly solo? Or as a crew? Depends on what you want.
- Fixed-wing offers more travel, time in the logbook, and (eventually) better pay.
- Many FW pilots prefer flying cargo instead of passengers.
- Your choice may rest on innate ability, and that's okay.
- It's feasible to purchase your own fixed-wing, less so a helicopter.

Lessons Chapter 5

- Single pilot or flying with company: It's a choice.
- Rookie jobs in either category can be dirty, depressing, and dangerous.
- Corporate aviation is lucrative, clean, and often boring.
- Imagine yourself in both cockpits and ask why you chose to fly.
- Do you want to fly? Or do you want others to see you flying?

Lessons Chapter 6
- Military flight school can expedite your career.
- A part 61 school may be cheaper but a 141 school may be better.
- Choosing a category is critical. FW or RW? Both have pluses and minuses.
- If/when a company sells the aircraft you've been flying, put copies of your resumé somewhere inside it. The buyer may need a pilot.
- If you learn of an upcoming flying slot and you don't want it for yourself, pass the information along to a fellow aviator. The gesture could repay you along the way.
- Crossing from military to commercial will be difficult. You'll adapt, but don't expect the two scenarios to be the same.
- Ref: my Toledo job, here are the lessons:
    1. A helicopter charter business will never work.
    2. Businesspeople think differently than pilots.
    3. Getting fired can be a great career boost.

Lessons Chapter 7
- Stretch the rules only with a damn good reason. Saving your aircraft and passengers is about the only one.

CHAPTER 18: FINAL REMARKS

- Keep your head on a swivel, always.
- It doesn't have to look pretty, just safe.
- Emergency? Slow down; it could save your life.
- Always fly first. Remember: Aviate, Navigate, Communicate.

Lessons Chapter 8
- Situational Awareness is a real thing. Trust it.
- If your gut says something's wrong, something's wrong.
- Aircraft don't magically fix themselves.
- Regardless of how good a job looks, sometimes it's
- advisable to walk away.
- You're not flying for pay; you're flying to build a legacy.
- Risk can never be zero; but it can be minimized.
- If it's bad on the ground, it will only get worse in the air.

Lessons Chapter 9
- If you're not aware of the beauty of flying, go back to work.
- No matter how many hours in the logbook, you'll always be a rookie, and that's a good thing.
- Big aircraft are fun; small aircraft can be more fun.
- Fly it to the ground. Never give up!
- The most important sequence: Aviate, Navigate, Communicate.

Lessons Chapter 10

- There will be low points.
- Never take your career for granted.
- A safe, accident free/incident free career is priceless—and achievable.
- When it's time to give it up, you will know.

Lessons Chapter 11

- Mechanics are your friends. Treat them well.
- The best way to treat a mechanic well is to treat the aircraft well.
- Describing the glitch precisely helps a lot. Write-ups for noises, and shimmies, and vibrations, and hiccups aren't helpful.
- Don't break rules, but don't bring your mechanic in at 3 a.m. to fix a burned out lightbulb, either. Change it yourself, or wait till morning.
- Help them with the work. You'll learn a lot.
- Take your mechanic flying when you can. They rarely ask, and few pilots offer.
- Don't boggle up the paperwork. (See the template)
- Never blame a mechanic for your screwup. Never.
- Pay attention to pending inspections. Don't overfly them.
- The mechanic has a license to protect, too.

CHAPTER 18: FINAL REMARKS

Lessons Chapter 12

- Listen to your passengers.
- Be the best pilot they've ever flown with.
- Pay attention to their physical needs.
- Never dismiss their fears.
- They rarely tell you everything, so ask.
- Body language is important.
- For unreasonable requests, use safety as a reason to say no.
- Don't be a cowboy, it impresses no one.

Lessons Chapter 13

- You may have to be selfish. Capturing your dream to fly is worth it.
- Don't be afraid to say no. Keep your head up.
- Check with the insurance provider about logged hours required.
- Don't be afraid to confront a cowboy pilot. You're flying an aircraft they've been flying, and your career could be on the line.
- Don't pad a logbook. Employers can sense inexperience.
- If you can't stay single, look for another pilot. He/She will understand better than a non-flyer.

- Have another useful skill to fall back on.
- No smoking, and No drugs!
- Wear hearing protection
- Get plenty of sleep and exercise.
- Pick up FOD.

Lessons Chapter 14

—CRM works. It will keep you safe. See it; say it; fix it.

Lessons Chapter 15

- Don't piss people off.
- The FAA is not out to get you.
- In aviation, knowledge = insurance. Stock up.
- Be a professional. It may cost you, but professionalism is more than worth it.

CHAPTER 18: FINAL REMARKS

CONCLUSION

We're on final approach, so I'll pass along a few more things. Notice in the book that I've included not just positive, encouraging, affirming comments, but the somewhat negative ones about aviation as well. After flying for fifty years, both in military and commercial aircraft, I can attest that aviation isn't all sweetness and light; it can be discouraging, dissatisfying, and disheartening. I meant what I said that at times I couldn't believe how little they paid me to fly. In every assignment there's a lingering belief by some—the public, the FAA, employers at times—that pilots don't just make a living in the air. Instead, you "get to fly". That mentality can limit your career by being a rationale for low compensation, uncertain/unequal benefits, and harsh working conditions.

I've always favored union membership and full participation in the aviation industry. A strong, engaged labor union might add an additional layer of bureaucracy, a bit more paperwork, and more cash from your paycheck for union dues. Unions also have a reputation, merited or not, for shielding poor performers, and for contributing to mediocrity. But a labor union can be the only protection between you and management.

Some of these lessons can be hard for you to hear, and harder to learn for a rookie pilot full of enthusiasm. My desire is not to discourage you, but to inform you. That's the purpose of this book. If you love to fly as much as I did, nothing will turn you away.

The dream to fly is as old as humankind. From the first time we watched an ancient bird leap into the sky, we've dreamt of doing likewise. The wish to become a pilot is an honorable one, and if you're truly destined to fly, there'll be no changing your mind.

In December 1903, on the windswept dunes at Kitty Hawk North Carolina, Orville Wright took off in the Wright flyer, and stayed aloft for twelve seconds. He flew 120 feet, about the wingspan of a 737. In the coming days, the Wrights flew again and again, and when they returned to Dayton, Ohio and home, their accomplishment was already known and lauded around the world, long before Facebook, Twitter, or Instagram. The message flew faster and farther than Orville did: We can fly!

I hope my book helps you attain your own flying dream, and that you achieve whatever aviation goal you have in mind. In the fifty years I was privileged to fly, I logged 12,500 hours in the air. That's 520 days in the cockpit, nearly a year and a half. It would have been longer, but my career was cut short when a medical issue put me on the ground. I was fifty-six-years old at the time, and nowhere near ready to quit flying. But then I would never have been entirely ready to quit. Here's a haiku

CHAPTER 18: FINAL REMARKS

from a fellow pilot whose experience closely matched my own, so his poem resonates with me:

> Thirty-eight years and
> Twenty-five thousand hours.
> I retired. Bye y'all.
>
> —CA Donald Steinman PHX (ret)
>
> —*From Beyond Haiku: Pilots Write Poetry by Capt. Linda Pauwels*[25]

I flew all over the world, in twenty-five different kinds of aircraft, doing dozens of flying jobs. I write "jobs", but the truth is that flying was never a *job* for me. I never worked a day in my life.

Chase your dream of a life in the sky. It's a fine way to live, and I highly recommend it. There'll be speed bumps, setbacks, and disappointments, of course. You'll get discouraged and disillusioned, especially at first. But keep going. If you were meant to fly, nothing will hold you back, and pursuing anything else will leave you wondering "what if?" Avoid that. Life's too short to work just for money, or to help someone else achieve *their* dream. Don't be afraid to be selfish, and to demand what you want. There's something to be said for aggressive people in aviation, too. Indeed, passivity is the last trait you should have.

Another piece of advice: Never be afraid to ask older pilots for advice, and to tell you their stories. Don't dismiss their history and exploits, assuming veteran pilots don't wish to be bothered. I can tell you that we don't mind. We love being asked. The challenge might be turning an old pilot off once she gets started. Any pilot will be grateful and happy to share stories with you.

One last comment: Take notes. Someday, sooner than you imagine, you'll retire from aviation, and you may want to write your own version of this book. Your notes will be valuable when you write your own *Postflight*.

Aviation is a disease for which there's no known cure. Until there is, happy flying, and keep the greasy side down. Make sure your takeoffs and landings equal out, and may you run out of time before you run out of sky.

Thank you for reading *Postflight: An Old Pilot's Logbook*.

—An old pilot

CHAPTER 18: FINAL REMARKS

RESOURCES

Part 141 Aviation Schools offering degree programs

Airline Transport Pilots
Locations: Several.
Training programs offered:
Airline Career Pilot Program
ATP Certification Training Program
904-595-7950/atpflightschools.com

Embry-Riddle.
Daytona Beach, FL and Prescott, AZ
Flight degree programs available:
Bachelors in Aeronautical Science.
800-522-6787/worldwide@erau.edu
Aero.und.edu/ 701-777-4934

Florida Institute of Technology
Melbourne, FL
Bachelor's degrees in:
Aeronautical Science
Aviation Management
Aviation Meteorology
(321) 674-8000/fit.edu

W Michigan University/College of aviation
Battle Creek, MI
Flight degree programs:
Bachelor's degrees in:
Aviation flight science
Air Force ROTC
Minor
Aviation science
Military leadership and aviation studies
(269) 964-6375/wmich.edu/aviation

U of North Dakota
Grand Forks, ND and Crookston, MN.
Bachelor's degrees in:
Air Traffic Management
Airport Management
Aviation Management
Aviation Studies
Commercial Aviation
Unmanned Aircraft System Operations

Minors available in:
Aviation Management
Professional Flight
Space Studies

CHAPTER 18: FINAL REMARKS

Ohio State University.

Columbus, OH

Degree programs: Bachelor's in Aviation & Air Transportation.

Aviation.osu.edu/ 614-292-2405

Purdue University.

West Lafayette, IN

Bachelor's degrees in:

Professional flight

Five-Year combined BS-MS program

Master's degrees in:

Aviation and Aerospace Management

Purdueaviationllc.com/ 765-743-9692

Saint Louis University (SLU)

St. Louis MO/Cahokia Illinois

Flight degree programs:

Bachelor's degrees in:

Aeronautics/Flight Science concentration.

Slu.edu/314-977-8203

San Jose State University

Flight degree programs:

Bachelor's degrees in:
Aviation – Professional Flight.
Sjsu.edu/408) 924-3190

Spartan College of Aeronautics and Technology
Tulsa, OK

Utah Valley University
Location: Orem, UT
Bachelor's degrees in:
Aviation – Professional Flight
Technology Management.
Uvu.edu/aviation/801-863-7830
Associate degrees in: Aviation

CHAPTER 18: FINAL REMARKS

ADDITIONAL RESOURCES:

- Advanced Air Flight School, DBA Carver Aero, Council Bluffs, Iowa, http://advancedaircb.com/flight-school/
- Angel Flight | People Flying People in Need
- Basic Aerobatics with Patty Wagstaff: https://pattywagstaff.com/
- Boldmethod.com
- Causey Aviation: https://www.causeyaviation.com/
- EAA: https://www.eaa.org/eaa/youth/free-ye-flights
- FlightGest Academy: https://www.flightgestacademy.com
- Epic Flight Academy: https://epicflightacademy.com/
- Evidence Based Training (ICAO) booklet: https://tinyurl.com/b6yvmjpb
- L3 Harris: https://www.l3commercialaviation.com/
- Miami-Dade College: https://www.mdc.edu/aviation/
- Ninety-Nines Professional Pilot Leadership Initiative
- https://tinyurl.com/yz37tdp9
- pilotmail.com
- https://www.ninety-nines.org/
- Paragonflight.com
- Pilotinstitute.com/
- PilotsnPaws: https://www.pilotsnpaws.org/guidelines/
- Sporty's Pilot Shop www.sportys.com
- United States Air Force Auxiliary | Civil Air Patrol National Headquarters

AVIATION SCHOLARSHIPS

- AAERO Aspiring pilot's scholarship
- https://www.aaero.com/aviation-scholarships/
- Aero Club of New England
- https://www.acone.org/scholarships
- Air Traffic Control Association
- https://www.atca.org/scholarship
- AOPA https://www.aopa.org/training-and-safety/students/flight-training-scholarships
- Amelia Earhart Scholarship via The 99s
- https://www.ninety-nines.org/scholarships.html
- AVscholars
- http://avscholars.com/
- AOPA Women in Aviation scholarships
- https://www.aopa.org/news-and-media/all-news/2010/august/03/new-scholarships-available-to-women
- Civil Air Patrol scholarships
- https://www.gocivilairpatrol.com/programs/cadets/cadetinvest
- Epic Flight Academy
- https://epicflightacademy.com/aviation-scholarship/
- Experimental Aircraft Association (EAA)
- https://www.eaa.org/eaa/youth/aviation-scholarships

CHAPTER 18: FINAL REMARKS

- Global Air Calvin Carrithers
- https://www.globalair.com/scholarships/
- Leroy Homer jr. http://leroywhomerjr.org/scholarships/
- Michigan Takes Flight http://michigantakesflight.org/
- Organization of Black Aerospace Professionals OBAP
- https://obap.org/
- Whirly Girls
- https://whirlygirls.org/
- Women in Aviation International
- https://www.wai.org/education/scholarships

I do not endorse any of the mentioned schools/resources, nor have I received endorsement or compensation from them. The information was accurate at this writing, but your experience may be different. As with all offerings, I encourage you as a prospective pilot/student to do thorough research, read testimonials and reviews, and get any financial and/or employment offers in writing.

FOOTNOTES

1. Army AFAST/SIFT: https://militaryflighttests.com/sift-practice-test/
2. *A Vietnam Anthem:* https://tinyurl.com/y3qhqx9j
3. Vietnam Magazine March 1990:
4. FAA Medical Clearance: https://www.faa.gov/licenses_certificates/medical_certification/
5. AOPA: https://www.aopa.org/
6. http://pilots.jetblue.com/
7. https://unitedaviate.com/
8. Link Trainer: https://www.wmof.com/c3link.html
9. MEL: https://tinyurl.com/y5vrgfrb
10. https://www.operationmilitarykids.org/army-helicopter-pilot-requirements/
11. FAA Approved part 141 flight training: https://tinyurl.com/y6hll39n
12. Operation Moccasin Bob Morris: https://www.comanchero.org/R_T_Moccasin_091470.htm
13. Bambi Bucket®: https://www.sei-ind.com/products/bambi-max/
14. Helicopters Incorporated: https://www.heliinc.com/
15. AOPA Wire Strike article: https://tinyurl.com/yyro3kdc
16. *The Sky Behind Me: A Memoir of Flying and Life:* https://tinyurl.com/yyjrwp7l

17. Hearing loss: https://www.aviationmedicine.com/article/hearing-loss/
18. Health Risks for Pilots: https://www.cdc.gov/niosh/topics/aircrew/default.html
19. Back strain in pilots: https://pubmed.ncbi.nlm.nih.gov/2954530/ https://pubmed.ncbi.nlm.nih.gov/15860899/
20. CRM: https://en.wikipedia.org/wiki/Crew_resource_management
21. FAA AD/SB: https://tinyurl.com/yxstjmh5
22. AOPA Pilot Protection Service: https://pilot-protection-services.aopa.org/about
23. Kobe Bryant S-76 accident: https://en.wikipedia.org/wiki/2020_Calabasas_helicopter_crash
24. *The Sky Behind Me, a Memoir of Flying and Life:* https://tinyurl.com/t9858yep
25. *Beyond Haiku: Pilots Write Poetry* Capt. Linda Pauwels: https://tinyurl.com/5dp5b9zz

GLOSSARY:

- AC—Aircraft Commander, pilot designation used in combat
- AD—Airworthiness Directive, issued by the FAA, a mandatory alert that grounds an aircraft until the AD addressed
- AFCS—Automatic Flight Control System, similar to an autopilot
- AK-47—Automatic weapon used by many Warsaw Pact nations
- AOPA—Aircraft Owners & Pilots Association
- APU—Auxiliary Power Unit
- A&P—Airframe & Powerplant (maintenance) certificate
- AS-350—AStar, single-engine helicopter now made by Airbus
- ATC—Air Traffic Control
- BambiBucket®—Fire-fighting water receptacle slung under a helicopter
- Bell—Bell Helicopter
- Bell 47—First commercial helicopter, the type of aircraft used on the M*A*S*H TV show, and 'Whirlybirds'
- Bell 222—Twin-engine corporate helicopter

CHAPTER 18: FINAL REMARKS

- CAVU—Ceiling And Visibility Unlimited
- CBP—Customs & Border Patrol
- CCN—Command & Control North, a cross-border mission during the Vietnam War
- Cessna 182 RG—Single-engine plane with retractable gear
- CH-47 Chinook—Heavy lift, tandem-rotor helicopter manufactured by Boeing
- Connie—Lockheed corporation L-1049 four-engine, propeller airplane. The Connie (also called the Constellation) flew for several airlines, most notably as the flagship of Trans World Airlines, TWA
- CPR—Cardiopulmonary Resuscitation
- CRM—Crew Resource Management
- ELT—Emergency Locator Transmitter
- EMT—Emergency Medical Technician
- ENG—Electronic News Gathering
- EP—Emergency Procedure
- FAR—Federal Air Regulations
- FAA—Federal Aviation Administration
- FBO—Fixed Base Operator, an airport manager/business
- FD&H—Fat, Dumb, and Happy, obliviousness in the cockpit. I always thought this would make a great aviation comic strip with three characters: Fatt, Dumm, & Happy. (It's yours, run with it)

- FOD—Foreign Object Damage
- Gouge—Information, the inside dope. Can be good or bad gouge.
- GPS—Global Positioning System
- HEMS—Helicopter Emergency Medical Services
- Hughes—Former manufacturer of small training helicopters
- Huey—UH-1, the main troop-transport helicopter used in the Vietnam War
- IFR—Instrument Flight Regulations/Rules
- IMC—Instrument Meteorological Conditions
- IP—Instructor Pilot
- Isobars—Lines of equal atmospheric pressure on weather charts
- Jet Ranger—Small, single-engine utility helicopter made by Bell, with capacity for a pilot and four passengers
- JFK Jr.—Son of President John F. Kennedy, JFK Jr. was killed in a plane crash in July 1999
- Kauai—Farthest west of the Hawaiian Islands
- Khe Sanh—location in Vietnam, site of bloody battles
- LongRanger—Slightly larger version of the Bell Jet Ranger, with capacity for a pilot and six passengers
- LZ—Landing Zone (a hot LZ indicates enemy presence)

CHAPTER 18: FINAL REMARKS

- MEL— Minimum Equipment List
- MTBF—Mean Time Between Failures, a metric used for critical parts, typically in turbine engines
- NG—National Guard
- NTSB—National Transportation Safety Board
- OTC—Over The Counter
- Part 61 School—Flight school at a local airport
- Part 141 School—Flight school designated solely for training
- PIC—Pilot In Command
- Pin flares—Small flares launched by hand to mark location
- PRC-90—Hand-held, military two-way radio
- Robinson R-22—Two-seat training helicopter
- RPG—Rocket Propelled Grenade
- SB—Service Bulletin—A notable maintenance issue. SBs are typically not grounding items
- Sikorsky—Large, multi-passenger helicopter
- WOFT—Warrant Officer Flight Trainee. Warrant Officers in the U.S. Army typically fly helicopters
- VFR—Visual Flight Regulations/Rules

BIBLIOGRAPHY

- *An Officer, Not a Gentleman.* ©2020 Mandy Hickson
- *Antenna Up, Crew Resource Management for Helicopter Pilots,* ©2017 Randy Mains https://tinyurl.com/3274nxhu
- *A Vietnam Anthem, What the War Gave Me* ©2016 Byron Edgington
- *Beyond Haiku: Pilots Write Poetry* ©2021 Captain Linda Pauwels CA Boeing 787
- *Buccaneer: The Provocative Odyssey of Jack Reed, Adventurer, Drug Smuggler and Pilot Extraordinaire* ©2013 MayCay Beeler & Jack Carlton Reed
- *CIA Superpilot Spills the Beans* ©2017 Bill Collier
- *Contact Flying* (Revised) ©2019 Jim Dulin
- EBT booklet: https://store.icao.int/en/manual-of-evidence-based-training-doc-9995
- *Ely Air Lines, Select Stories from 10 Years of a Weekly Column,* ©2020 Mike and Linda Street-Ely
- *Finding Amelia:* Lynsey Howell https://www.amazon.com/Finding-Amelia-Lynsey-Howell/dp/1631775790
- *Flight To Success be the Captain of Your Life,* ©2015 and the Aviation "Flight For" Thriller Series. Karlene Pettit PhD, MBA, MHS
- *From Plain to Plane, My Mennonite Childhood, A*

CHAPTER 18: FINAL REMARKS

National Scandal, and an Unconventional Soar to Freedom ©2021 Patty Bear
- *Latinas in Aviation* ©2021 Jacqueline Ruiz
- *Panama's Gold** ©2020 Jim Tritten, & Sandi Hoover Melting Pot Anthology *1st place winner, New Mexico Press Women's annual communications contest
- *The Fig Factor* Jacqueline Camacho-Ruiz https://tinyurl.com/2ar4w9ub
- *The Grit Factor,* ©2020 Shannon Huffman-Polson
- *The Sky Behind Me, a Memoir of Flying and Life* ©2012 Byron Edgington
- *Touch the Sky* ©2010 Sandi Pierce Browne
- *The Happy Bottom Riding Club* ©2000 Lauren Kessler
- *Wind, Sand and Stars,* ©1939 Antoine de St. Exupéry
- Aviatrix Book Reviews. A source for almost any topic in aviation, focusing on women in the cockpit. https://aviatrixbookreview.com/

ABOUT THE AUTHOR

Byron Edgington was a commercial and military helicopter pilot for fifty years. An award-winning writer, he is the author of several books including *The Sky Behind Me: A Memoir of Flying and Life*, *A Vietnam Anthem: What the War Gave Me*, *Waiting for Willie Pete, a Novel of Vietnam*, and *Postflight: An Old Pilot's Logbook*.

Edgington served in the US Army as a helicopter pilot, including a yearlong tour in Vietnam. After retiring from aviation, he returned to college, and received his bachelor's degree in English and creative writing from The Ohio State University. In 2012, Edgington won the prestigious Bailey Prize in prose from the Swedenborg Foundation Press for his essay titled, *Lift Off*.

Edgington is married to his best friend, Mariah. He has three daughters, and five grandchildren. He lives in Iowa City Iowa. The author's books, including *Postflight, An Old Pilot's Logbook*, are available at Amazon in print and digital editions, through your local independent bookstore or library, or at www.Byronedgington.com and www.figfactormedia.com

CHAPTER 18: FINAL REMARKS

If you enjoyed this book, and found it useful, please consider:

- Writing a customer review.
- Gift a copy to someone who might benefit from reading it.
- Share a photo of the cover/title on social media.
- Suggest *Postflight: An Old Pilot's Logbook* to your book club.
- Donate a copy of *Postflight* to the library when you become a pilot.
- If you have a blog or podcast, mention *PostFlight* there.
- Contact me for an interview.
- Use these hashtags when writing about *PostFlight*: #Aviationtraining, #aviationcareers, #aviation, #flying, #Postflight:anoldpilotslogbook.
- Please contact author for information on bulk orders.

MORE BY THIS AUTHOR:

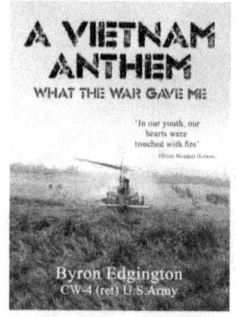

A Vietnam Anthem describes what effects the war in South East Asia had on its author, and the man he became afterward, both good and bad. The war in Vietnam was a national tragedy. The author carries a lot of ambivalence about it, because, as horrible as his participation in the war was, it gave him a gratifying career in commercial aviation. https://tinyurl.com/24jxbfs6

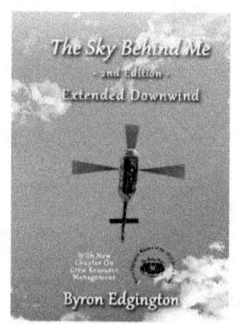

The Sky Behind Me, a Memoir of Flying and Life is the author's personal recollections of a life in the sky, and his memories from the cockpit. For forty years the author flew helicopters all over the world, both commercially & in the military. He doused forest fires in Alaska, counted power poles in Ohio, reported news and traffic in several large American cities, and for twenty years he rescued ill and injured medical patients while based at a hospital in Iowa. TSBM details a life lived in the generous, beautiful, always challenging, and often dangerous sky. https://tinyurl.com/5du4r8na

CHAPTER 18: FINAL REMARKS

Waiting for Willie Pete is a helicopter novel of Vietnam. Based on *Moby Dick, Waiting for Willie Pete* is a tale of desperation, obsession, danger, and the vicissitudes of war. Filled with Melvillean characters modeled on men the author flew with in combat—Captain A'Hearn, Piper, Starkey, Stebbins, Fisk, and more, it's a stark portrayal of what the Vietnam war was truly like, especially for helicopter crews. As Sergeant Quillig says, 'war is not on fields of battle; war is in the minds and hearts of men.' https://tinyurl.com/ww5dc

All books are available on Amazon, or through the author's website: **www.byronedgington.com**

www.ingramcontent.com/pod-product-compliance
Lightning Source LLC
LaVergne TN
LVHW052340080426
835508LV00045B/2882